Understanding World History

The
Enlightenment

Other titles in the series include:

Ancient Chinese Dynasties
Ancient Egypt
Ancient Greece
Ancient Rome
The Black Death
The Decade of the 2000s
The Digital Age
The Early Middle Ages
Elizabethan England
The Great Recession
The History of Rock and Roll
The History of Slavery
The Holocaust
The Industrial Revolution
The Late Middle Ages
The Making of the Atomic Bomb
Pearl Harbor
The Renaissance
The Rise of Islam
The Rise of the Nazis
Victorian England

Understanding World History

The Enlightenment

Toney Allman

Bruno Leone
Series Consultant

ReferencePoint Press®

San Diego, CA

940.2
ALL

For more information, contact:
ReferencePoint Press, Inc.
PO Box 27779
San Diego, CA 92198
www.ReferencePointPress.com

Picture credits:
Cover: Jean-Baptiste Colbert (1619-83) Presenting the Members of the Royal Academy of Science to Louis XIV (1638–1715) c.1667 (oil on canvas) (detail) (see also 104626), Testelin, Henri (1616–95)/Château de Versailles, France/Giraudon/Bridgeman Images
Maury Aaseng: 12
© Bettmann/Corbis: 24, 63
© Julian Calder/Corbis: 78
© The Print Collector/Corbis: 31, 72
Thinkstock Images: 8, 9
Ambrogio Lorenzetti (1280–1348). Effects of Good Government in the city. Fresco. Detail. Merchants in the walled city of Siena./Photo © Tarker/Bridgeman Images: 18
Voltaire (hand-coloured etching), French School, (18th century)/Bibliotheque Nationale, Paris, France/Bridgeman Images: 37
The Oath of Horatii, 1784 (oil on canvas), David, Jacques Louis (1748–1825)/Louvre, Paris, France/Giraudon/Bridgeman Images: 43
Plate showing rhinoceros and elephant, Engraving from Denis Diderot, Jean Baptiste Le Rond d'Alembert, L'Encyclopedie, 1751–1757 Entitled Histoire Naturelle, Regne animal series (Natural History, Animal Kingdom) Drawing by Martinet, engraving by Bernard/De Agostini Picture Library/Bridgeman Images: 48
Second Table of the Linnean Plant Sexual System (coloured engraving), Linnaeus, Carl (1707–78)/Bibliotheque des Arts Decoratifs, Paris, France/Archives Charmet/Bridgeman Images: 53
Equestrian Portrait of Catherine II (1729–96) the Great of Russia (oil on canvas), Erichsen, Vigilius (1722–82)/Musee des Beaux-Arts, Chartres, France/Bridgeman Images: 58
Execution of Louis XVI (1754–93) 21st January 1793 (coloured engraving) (see also 14664), French School, (18th century)/Bibliotheque Nationale, Paris, France/Bridgeman Images: 68

LIBRARY OF CONGRESS CATALOGING-IN-PUBLICATION DATA

Allman, Toney.
    The enlightenment / by Toney Allman.
      pages cm. -- (Understanding world history series)
    Includes bibliographical references and index.
    ISBN 978-1-60152-740-0 (hardback) -- ISBN 1-60152-740-3 (hardback)
    1. Enlightenment--Europe--Juvenile literature. 2. Europe--History--18th century--Juvenile literature.
3. Europe--Intellectual life--18th century--Juvenile literature. 4. Enlightenment--United States--
Juvenile literature. 5. United States--Intellectual life--18th century--Juvenile literature. I. Title.
    D286.A45   2015
    940.2'53--dc23
                                                      2014019967

Contents

Foreword

When the Puritans first emigrated from England to America in 1630, they believed that their journey was blessed by a covenant between themselves and God. By the terms of that covenant they agreed to establish a community in the New World dedicated to what they believed was the true Christian faith. God, in turn, would reward their fidelity by making certain that they and their descendants would always experience his protection and enjoy material prosperity. Moreover, the Lord guaranteed that their land would be seen as a shining beacon—or in their words, a "city upon a hill"—that the rest of the world would view with admiration and respect. By embracing this notion that God could and would shower his favor and special blessings upon them, the Puritans were adopting the providential philosophy of history—meaning that history is the unfolding of a plan established or guided by a higher intelligence.

The concept of intercession by a divine power is only one of many explanations of the driving forces of world history. Historians and philosophers alike have subscribed to numerous other ideas. For example, the ancient Greeks and Romans argued that history is cyclical. Nations and civilizations, according to these ancients of the Western world, rise and fall in unpredictable cycles; the only certainty is that these cycles will persist throughout an endless future. The German historian Oswald Spengler (1880–1936) echoed the ancients to some degree in his controversial study *The Decline of the West.* Spengler asserted that all civilizations inevitably pass through stages comparable to the life span of a person: childhood, youth, adulthood, old age, and, eventually, death. As the title of his work implies, Western civilization is currently entering its final stage.

Joining those who see purpose and direction in history are thinkers who completely reject the idea of meaning or certainty. Rather, they reason that since there are far too many random and unseen factors at work on the earth, historians would be unwise to endorse historical predictability of any type. Warfare (both nuclear and conventional), plagues, earthquakes, tsunamis, meteor showers, and other catastrophic world-changing events have loomed large throughout history and prehistory. In his essay "A Free Man's Worship," philosopher and mathematician

Bertrand Russell (1872–1970) supported this argument, which many refer to as the nihilist or chaos theory of history. According to Russell, history follows no preordained path. Rather, the earth itself and all life on earth resulted from, as Russell describes it, an "accidental collocation of atoms." Based on this premise, he pessimistically concluded that all human achievement will eventually be "buried beneath the debris of a universe in ruins."

Whether history does or does not have an underlying purpose, historians, journalists, and countless others have nonetheless left behind a record of human activity tracing back nearly 6,000 years. From the dawn of the great ancient Near Eastern civilizations of Mesopotamia and Egypt to the modern economic and military behemoths China and the United States, humanity's deeds and misdeeds have been and continue to be monitored and recorded. The distinguished British scholar Arnold Toynbee (1889–1975), in his widely acclaimed twelve-volume work entitled *A Study of History,* studied twenty-one different civilizations that have passed through history's pages. He noted with certainty that others would follow.

In the final analysis, the academic and journalistic worlds mostly regard history as a record and explanation of past events. From a more practical perspective, history represents a sequence of building blocks—cultural, technological, military, and political—ready to be utilized and enhanced or maligned and perverted by the present. What that means is that all societies—whether advanced civilizations or preliterate tribal cultures—leave a legacy for succeeding generations to either embrace or disregard.

Recognizing the richness and fullness of history, the ReferencePoint Press Understanding World History series fosters an evaluation and interpretation of history and its influence on later generations. Each volume in the series approaches its subject chronologically and topically, with specific focus on nations, periods, or pivotal events. Primary and secondary source quotations are included, along with complete source notes and suggestions for further research.

Moreover, the series reflects the truism that the key to understanding the present frequently lies in the past. With that in mind, each series title concludes with a legacy chapter that highlights the bonds between past and present and, more important, demonstrates that world history is a continuum of peoples and ideas, sometimes hidden but there nonetheless, waiting to be discovered by those who choose to look.

Important Events of the Enlightenment

1687
Isaac Newton publishes *Principia Mathematica*, thereby revolutionizing humankind's understanding of the workings of the universe.

1756
The Seven Years' War begins between England and France. In America this global conflict is known as the French and Indian War.

1752
The first condemnation of the *Encyclopédie* occurs.

1730
John Wesley and Charles Wesley found Methodism in Oxford, England.

1700   **1720**   **1740**   **1760**

1693
John Locke publishes *Thoughts Concerning Education*, in which he describes infants as being born as "blank slates."

1751
The first volume of Denis Diderot and Jean le Rond d'Alembert's *Encyclopédie* is published.

1755
A major earthquake strikes Lisbon, Portugal.

1718
Yale University is founded in Connecticut.

1759
Voltaire writes *Candide*.

1760
George III becomes king of Great Britain.

1776
The American Declaration of Independence is written, primarily by Thomas Jefferson.

1790
Edmund Burke publishes *Reflections on the Revolution in France.*

1786
Wolfgang Amadeus Mozart's opera *The Marriage of Figaro* is first performed.

1775
The American War of Independence begins.

| 1760 | 1770 | 1780 | 1790 | 1800 |

1781
Immanuel Kant publishes *The Critique of Pure Reason.*

1789
The French Revolution begins.

1793
The French Reign of Terror begins.

1762
Catherine the Great becomes empress of Russia.

1794
Thomas Paine writes *The Age of Reason*, in which he challenges organized religion and Christianity and advocates reason and Deism.

The Defining Characteristics of the Enlightenment

The Enlightenment was in general a philosophical movement of eighteenth-century Europe and the Americas. The era is also referred to as the Age of Reason because its philosophy embraced the idea that humanity could progress and improve through the use of reason and rationality, as opposed to tradition, authority, faith, or religious dogma. Historians disagree about the exact dates, but the period lasted roughly from 1685 to 1815. The philosophy of the Enlightenment had a radical effect on religion, politics, science, literature, and the arts.

Goals and Limitations

The goal of the Enlightenment's leaders and proponents was intellectual freedom and the liberation of the individual from any authority other than each person's thoughtful reasoning, but in reality this philosophy was not as democratic as it sounded. For the most part Enlightenment thinkers were elitists who believed in freedom for the educated, academic, thoughtful people able to reason for themselves. They were white, male, and of the middle and upper classes of their societies. They were academics, wealthy people, or aristocrats. Immanuel Kant—one of the major philosophers of the time—thought most other classes of people made up "the great unthinking masses." These masses were uneducated working-class people or peasants who, Kant believed, did not know how to think for themselves and could not be expected to do so. Kant and most other Enlightenment thinkers felt the same way about women. Kant claimed that using reason to make decisions was believed to be "very dangerous by the far greater portion of mankind (and by the entire fair sex.)"[1]

Just as women were believed to be too emotional and nonintellectual to use reason, so too were people of color. Enlightenment philosopher David Hume, for example, assumed that other races were primitive and not as intelligent or as evolved as white men. Enlightened thinkers, however, did not blame non-European races for their perceived deficiencies. Modern day philosopher Kieron O'Hara explains, "They felt that though non-whites were inferior and savage, this was not their fault."[2] People of color, women, and the masses would all benefit and be uplifted, said Enlightenment theory, by living in a liberal society guided by reason.

Major Enlightenment Ideas: The Individual

Despite the shortcomings of Enlightenment thinking, for its time the philosophy of individual freedom from authority and the supremacy of reason was radical and revolutionary. Enlightenment meant different things to different people, often depending on where in Europe or America they lived, but many modern historians do identify key defining characteristics of Enlightenment philosophy.

First, Enlightenment thinking focused on the individual—not outside authority—as the way to justify beliefs and behavior. This was an extremely progressive approach to life for most eighteenth-century societies. As an example, before the Enlightenment era, people believed that their king had been chosen by God and derived from Him the authority to rule. The king (or queen) had the right to demand unquestioning loyalty and obedience, and rebelling against the monarch's decrees was a terrible crime against God as well as the state. This concept is known as the divine right of kings. Religion provided another outside authority that required unquestioning obedience: People could

Europe in 1721

Kingdom of Norway
Kingdom of Sweden
Finland
St. Petersburg
NORTH SEA
Stockholm
RUSSIAN EMPIRE
Estonia
Kingdom of Denmark
Copenhagen
Grand Duchy of Lithuania
Dublin
Ireland
United Kingdom of Great Britain
Prussia
POLISH-LITHUANIAN COMMONWEALTH
England
United Netherlands
Brandenburg
Berlin
Warsaw
London
Amsterdam
ATLANTIC OCEAN
HOLY ROMAN EMPIRE
Dresden
Kingdom of Poland
Paris
Kingdom of Bohemia
Kingdom of France
Vienna
Moldova
Switzerland
Austria
Geneva
Venice
Kingdom of Hungary
Transylvania
Genoa
Wallachia
Republic of Genoa
Papal States
Venetian Republic
Bucharest
Kingdom of Portugal
Lisbon
Madrid
Tuscany
Montegnegro
Constantinople
Rome
OTTOMAN EMPIRE
Kingdom of Spain
Kingdom of Sardinia
Kingdom of Naples
MEDITERRANEAN SEA
Kingdom of Sicily
AFRICA

not doubt religious dogma or decree, whether biblical or ordered by the Catholic pope, or a minister, or merely church tradition. Such doubt was heretical and sinful.

By contrast, Enlightenment thinking rejected any authority other than the individual's own intelligence, experiences, and philosophy of life. Neither the divine right of kings nor religious dogma was more legitimate than an individual's freedom of thought. So individual psychology, self-interest as a moral pursuit, and the study of humanity became legitimate as well.

Optimism and Skepticism

Another defining characteristic of Enlightenment thinking was its optimism. Its philosophers commonly believed that humans are basically good, worthwhile as individuals, and capable of thinking for themselves; and that everything about the world is knowable and explainable. Society as a whole could make continual progress because all problems were solvable through the use of science, reason, and enlightened thinking. God had created a perfect world and given humankind the ability to understand that world. Enlightenment scientist Joseph Priestley expressed this optimism and confidence in his vision of the future. He said, "Men will make their situation in this world abundantly more easy and comfortable, they will probably prolong their existence in it, and will grow daily more happy. . . . Thus, whatever was the beginning of this world, the end will be glorious and paradisiacal, beyond what our imaginations can now conceive."[3]

At the same time that people were optimistic about human capabilities, however, enlightened thinkers insisted that each individual should question everything and take nothing on faith. Skepticism was another important aspect of Enlightenment philosophy. Just as enlightened individuals were skeptical about the divine right of kings or religious dogma, so they were skeptical of the enlightened thoughts of others—including their optimism. Enlightened thinkers questioned and disagreed with each other about each aspect of what being enlightened meant to them. They wondered who was truly enlightened and how that could be determined. They questioned each other's conclusions about the world, about humanity, and about science and reason. Skepticism became so extreme that some philosophers mocked the optimism of other Enlightenment leaders.

Reason

Skepticism about traditional authority was a defining characteristic of the Enlightenment, but something had to take the place of authority. That something was universal reason. Reason was the way to observe and understand the world—it was natural and reality-based—and the only proper source of authority. Enlightenment philosophers theorized that everyone had the same ability to reason and could discover the same universal truths by using reason. Universal reason was the path by which people could agree on universal truths. In other words, reason led to truth, and truth was of supreme value. Reasoning people should not believe anything that authorities asserted unless one's own reason showed the statement to be the truth. It did not matter if reason led to inconvenient or dangerous truths. It did not matter if the Church or the government did not like the truth. Uncovering these truths by the use of reason was the moral responsibility of every enlightened individual.

Because reason was the ultimate way to understand humanity and how the world worked, enlightened thinkers rejected blind faith in religion, in authorities, and in social traditions. Most Enlightenment leaders discarded belief in miracles, sneered at superstitions, and dismissed mysticism or folklore as unenlightened. They refused to accept that religious leaders or monarchs should be obeyed as sources of truth. They argued that each person should figure out reality and truth for himself and prove to his own satisfaction what was true or real.

A New Worldview

With their philosophy of reason and the importance of the individual, Enlightenment thinkers and leaders were not simply engaging in intellectual exercises. They were shaking the foundations of society and culture. They were throwing out old social constructs, doubting civilization's underpinnings, searching for definitive truth, and aspiring to perfecting the human condition. They saw their era as bringing light where before there had been only darkness. They were establishing a way of thinking that would affect every aspect of how people lived their lives.

Chapter 1

What Conditions Led to the Enlightenment?

I n Europe, religion and aristocratic authority controlled society for hundreds of years. Education and literacy were uncommon; people submitted to the domination of ancient knowledge, religious teachings, and the nobility. As the centuries passed, however, a few educated philosophers, scientists, and reformers began to question old ways. Literacy and education spread. Wealth, exploration, and trade with other cultures expanded. New ideas, knowledge, and experiences were the influences that eventually led to the age of the Enlightenment.

The Middle Ages

From the Middle Ages, which lasted from about 476 to roughly 1450 CE, came the beginnings of modern Europe. Medieval historians Judith M. Bennett and C. Warren Hollister explain, "During the Middle Ages, Europe grew from a predominantly rural society, thinly settled and impoverished, into a powerful and distinctive civilization whose history helped to shape the world we now know."[4] The distinctive society that developed in Europe during the Middle Ages was a Christian one, so much so that people thought of themselves as a part of Christendom rather than as citizens of a nation or a state. It was also a feudal society under a manorial system.

Feudalism was a political and military system under which a

The Renaissance Man

Leonardo da Vinci, who lived from 1452 to 1519, is often considered to be the epitome of the Renaissance man because he had many and varied intellectual interests and was an expert in several different disciplines. Mostly self-educated, da Vinci was a remarkable artist, a student of science and nature, an inventor, and a philosopher. Among other endeavors, da Vinci dissected human bodies that he secretly took from the morgue so that he could learn about and describe human anatomy; he studied the flight of birds to understand how they fly and drew up plans for a flying machine; he explored geology and fossils and theorized that shell fossils were the remains of living organisms that had once been under an ocean; he explored mathematics, physics, architecture, and astronomy; and he came up with ideas for military armament, such as steam-powered guns and a tank. Most of his ideas were never published or appreciated in his time, but he is recognized today as a true genius. His artistic virtuosity is most recognized in his paintings, including the *Mona Lisa* and the *Last Supper*. In later times the psychoanalyst Sigmund Freud remarked, "Leonardo da Vinci was like a man who awoke too early in the darkness, while the others were all still asleep."

Quoted in Kathy A. Miles and Charles F. Peters II, "Leonardo da Vinci: The Man, the Genius," StarrySkies.com, 2001. http://starryskies.com.

landowning elite—the nobility—ruled all the rest of the people. In feudal society a king or overlord divided the land he governed into large tracts called fiefs. These fiefs were ceded to nobles or lords who were vassals of the overlord. A vassal is a noble who owns land given to him in exchange for his promises of loyalty to the overlord or king. The few members of the landed nobility lived well for their times, in great castles or manor houses, and controlled much of the land in Europe.

The lord of the manor (who owned and controlled the fief) could be an aristocrat or noble, but he also might be an elite member of the clergy. In medieval times, Christianity was unified under the institution of the Catholic Church. Many lords were bishops of the Church, and the pope, who headed the Church, owned vast tracts of land. During the Middle Ages land was wealth, and both the nobility and the Church were extremely wealthy and powerful. They also controlled the vast majority of people who lived on and worked their lands.

The manorial system was the economic system concurrent with feudalism. It defined the relationship between the lords of the manor and the rest of the people. The "manor" was the lord's manor or castle along with one or more villages that made up the fief and all the surrounding lands of the estate. Peasants and serfs lived in the villages under the control of the manor. These people worked for the lord in return for the right to live in the village and work small pieces of land for themselves. They were under the protection and control of the lord of the manor, and if they were serfs, they were little better than slaves because they belonged to the lord. All the peasants were governed by the lord, but the serfs had few rights and were not even able to leave the estate without permission. Their labor was the rent they paid to the lord for their huts and the gardens they tended for food. They rarely had hope of bettering their lives.

The Medieval Church

For much of the Middle Ages, people were born into and belonged to one of three classes. They were aristocrats, clergy, or common people. The manorial system was a rigid hierarchy of classes, in which the Catholic Church taught that one's status was ordained by God. Morality and God's will were determined by the Church, which informed people and society as a whole what was right and how they must live. Even kings submitted to the dictates of Church laws.

The Middle Ages were an age of faith, perhaps in part because only

Merchants hawk their wares in the walled Italian city of Siena during the late Middle Ages. A distinctive civilization developed in Europe during the medieval period.

through religion could people make sense of the world. Throughout most of the Middle Ages people had no knowledge of natural laws or why events occurred. They did not know how to explain disasters such as earthquakes, floods, droughts, famines, epidemics of diseases, or life and death. Bennett and Hollister say that their world was full of "uncertainties, mysteries, and demons."[5] God was all powerful, but unknowable, and might punish sinners with diseases or disasters as easily as protect people from unseen evil forces. When disaster struck without warning, it was often seen as God's punishment. When disease struck, its victim might get well or die for no apparent reason other than God's will. Religion provided the only explanations that people had for the unpredictable events in their lives. The Church offered the only safety in an uncertain and inexplicable world. For most people religion was superstitious and mystical, and they depended on Church leaders to tell them how to please God and how to avoid His almost capricious vengeance.

A Reasoning Faith

As the Middle Ages progressed, especially by the thirteenth and fourteenth centuries, great social changes began to occur. Towns and cities grew, trade and technology advanced, and with them a new social class developed—the middle class. These people were not nobles or clergy, but they acquired wealth and status. They sought the education and literacy that had previously been available only to a few of the aristocracy and the clergy. Universities were established, and both nobles and middle-class citizens took advantage of them. Some Catholic schools and universities taught theology (the study of religion) as more spiritual and rational than superstitious and mystical. Interest in philosophy, science, literature, and logic developed. While remaining intensely religious, some scholars and academics began to question established theology and interpretations of religion that seemed to lack reason.

In the late thirteenth century, for example, Thomas Aquinas, a priest and philosopher, wrote a famous book, *Summa Theologica*, in which he details five logical proofs of the existence of God. Thomas Aquinas believed that God gave reason to people for a purpose, and that was to be able to be close to God using reason instead of relying on faith alone. Roger Bacon was another religious man who rejected the blind following of Church teachings. Instead, he argued, people should use their own observations to understand the world. He said that people should use experiments to "confirm, refute, or challenge theoretical claims"[6] about how the natural world works. He advocated questioning accepted theories such as ideas about why natural disasters happen, even if the Church's doctrine was that God decreed these events.

Despite the fact that men like Bacon and Aquinas were quite religious, the leaders of the Church rejected their ideas as against established Church dogma. During the Middle Ages the Catholic Church was intolerant of any thought or science that seemed to contradict its traditions, and it often dealt harshly with any unbelievers. Bacon, for example, was condemned and imprisoned for twelve years for suggesting that the world should be understood through science instead of faith. The charge against him was "on account of certain suspected novelties"[7] in his teachings about religion. For most people, then, including the clergy, the Middle Ages remained a period of faith and mysticism with supernatural explanations for the natural world.

The Middle Ages came to an end when the deadly bubonic plague swept through Europe during the fourteenth century, killing perhaps 25 million people, and the Hundred Years War between France and England devastated Europe's economy and disrupted the lives of its people. By the time the war ended in 1453, another 2 to 3 million people had died. Despite the tragedies of war and plague, Europe's civilization did recover, and the knowledge and ideas developed during the Middle Ages were not lost. The scholars and literate peoples of Europe began to look to the past to create a better world for themselves.

The Renaissance Era

From the last half of the fifteenth century through the seventeenth century, Europe entered the era known as the Renaissance. "Renaissance" means rebirth or reawakening, and the age was not only a rebirth of learning and interest in intellectual discovery, it was also a time of geographical discovery, increased trade, and political reorganization. Looking back to the great classical civilizations of antiquity for inspiration, Renaissance leaders wanted to reshape their world in the model of the

Religious Persecutions

Institutionalized religious persecutions, sanctioned by the Catholic Church and monarchal governments, were a fact of life from the thirteenth to the eighteenth centuries. Pope Gregory IX established the first Inquisition, or religious court, in 1233, which was a tribunal to bring to account anyone accused of heresy. Punishments for heresy could include imprisonment, beatings and torture, burning at the stake, confiscation of property, and exile or banishment from public life. The Inquisition spread throughout central and western Europe and even into the Americas, omitting only England and Scandinavia. Christians and Jews were accused and attacked as heretics whenever they held any religious view that was seen as opposed to Church dogma and traditional Christian teachings. At least six hundred thousand people were killed during Europe's Inquisition. Books deemed heretical were banned, and anyone owning such a book was arrested and punished. During the Reformation, when Protestantism was taking hold in Europe, religious wars broke out as the Catholic Church fought to retain its hold on power and eradicate the Protestants from Europe. Religious conflicts included civil wars and rebellions in France and in the Netherlands in the sixteenth century, a war between Spain and England in the sixteenth century, and Europe's Thirty Years' War in the seventeenth century. The terrors and evils of religious persecutions did not die out until the middle of the eighteenth century with the spread of Enlightenment ideas.

ancient Greek and Roman worlds. They rediscovered and read ancient literature, such as the works of the philosophers Aristotle and Plato. They modeled their art and literature after that of the Greeks and Romans and valued beauty and creativity.

The major intellectual and cultural movement of the Renaissance was the philosophy of humanism. Humanism was based on the belief that Greek and Roman writings contained everything that people need to know to live a moral and fulfilling life. It is a philosophy that places the highest value on human beings, their achievements, and their possibilities, as opposed to the spiritual, mystical mindset of medieval scholars. Humanists subscribe to the theory that people's thoughts and the rational evidence that they acquire during their lives are more worthwhile than is blind faith or memorized religious doctrine. Thus, classical literature was as important a part of education as was theology. Scholars and intellectuals became more secular (worldly and nonreligious) in their studies and became imaginative, creative, and excited about the possibilities of discoveries that human curiosity permitted. Rather than emphasizing spiritual life after death, they celebrated what people could achieve in the here and now. This approach did not mean that Renaissance people rejected religion. On the contrary, most Renaissance leaders were Christian and deeply religious, but they rejected the idea that religious tradition was the only truth.

Humanism's Beginnings

Renaissance thinkers believed that their new view of the world was a break with medieval thought, but in reality their humanistic philosophy began in the Middle Ages. Francesco Petrarch, an Italian clergyman, poet, and scholar of the early fourteenth century, was actually the world's first humanist. He studied the ancient works of the Roman orator Cicero and came to admire both his philosophy and his speaking skills. Petrarch once wrote a letter to "Posterity," describing himself as he wished to be remembered. It says, in part, "I possessed a well-balanced rather than a keen intellect, one prone to all kinds of good and wholesome study, but especially inclined to moral philosophy and the art of poetry. . . . Among the many subjects which interested me, I dwelt especially upon antiquity, for our own age has always repelled me, so that, had it not been for the love of those dear to me, I should have preferred to have been born in any other period than our own. In order to forget my own time, I have constantly striven to place myself in spirit in other ages, and consequently I delighted in history."[8]

At a time when most people were either illiterate or found reading or writing hard work, Petrarch had a passion for writing about and analyzing his thoughts and feelings. Human struggles and emotions absorbed him, and he considered the human intellect, human creativity, and the power of the human spirit to be legitimate paths to understanding God, the purpose of life, and the natural world. He valued humanity and its achievements, and he believed that individuals ought to think for themselves, transform society through education and philosophy, and uplift the culture of Europe. Even centuries after Petrarch's death, so great was his influence on the Renaissance that his works were studied and his sonnets were copied by the great Renaissance playwright and poet William Shakespeare.

The Humanistic Call for Reform

The exciting humanist philosophy of the Renaissance spread rapidly throughout Europe and affected many aspects of life. Literacy and education expanded, as did curiosity and an enthusiasm for discoveries about the world. Perhaps the most influential humanist philosopher, Desiderius Erasmus, was a Dutch Catholic priest who was called "The Prince of the Humanists."[9] Erasmus was a dedicated teacher, writer, and reformer. In 1509 he wrote a famous text, *The Praise of Folly*, which harshly criticized superstitious religious practices such as rich men making large donations to the Church to buy indulgences in order to reduce their time in Purgatory after death. He made fun of the clergy who took vows of poverty and then lived wealthy lives. He complained that Church leaders used their worldly authority to tyrannize the common people. He said of aristocratic nobles and courtiers who advised kings that they were "corrupt, servile, stupid, and cringing, and yet they wish to appear superior to all others."[10] Erasmus's humanism was a struggle against the evils of the Church, which had become corrupt in its use of earthly power. It attacked the state for its negligence of the people it was supposed to serve. It was a call for true Christian virtue and the use of reason to achieve morality.

The Polish astronomer Nicolaus Copernicus challenged Church doctrine. He proposed that the sun, rather than the earth, is the center of the universe.

Other humanists also found themselves at odds with the Church. The Polish astronomer Nicolaus Copernicus, who lived from 1473 to 1543, challenged Church doctrine in a revolutionary way. The Church taught that the earth was the center of God's universe. Copernicus proposed the theory that the sun is the center of the universe, all of the planets orbit the sun, and stars do not really move but only appear to because the earth is moving. Copernicus's heliocentric system appalled most religious people. One minister said, "This fool wants to turn the whole art of astronomy upside down."[11] Copernicus died shortly after his theories became public, and the Church banned his works.

An Age of Exploration and Discovery

Copernicus was criticized and rejected even by most of the scientists of his time, but in other ways, Renaissance explorers, discoverers, and scientists were generally eager to expand their knowledge of the world. They celebrated the potential of human achievement in their activities and were no longer willing to accept the incurious stagnation of medieval culture or the medieval Church. From the fifteenth through the seventeenth centuries, the Renaissance was an Age of Discovery. During this period Europeans ventured to the so-called New World of the Americas. The explorer Bartolomeu Dias sailed to the tip of Africa and thus discovered that the Atlantic Ocean and the Indian Ocean were connected. Portuguese explorer Vasco Da Gama then discovered the ocean route from Europe to India. Finally, Portuguese explorer Ferdinand Magellan led an expedition that sailed around the world in the sixteenth century, not only proving the theory that the world is round but also allowing geographers to map the globe.

Europe's global explorations marked the beginning of its expansionism and world dominance. In North and South America, in India, and in Africa, European expeditions conquered native peoples and established colonies of Europeans. The explorations and colonies led to vastly increased trade and wealth for Europe. Gold, diamonds, and slaves represented just some of the valuable commodities that poured into Europe during this time. The far-flung network of communications, trade, and commerce increased Europe's knowledge about the world, along with its increased wealth and the resultant rise in leisure time. It created an atmosphere in which the elites of European society had time for intellectual pursuits and the freedom to question the power of the Church and to challenge the tyranny of traditional teachings. Even though most people remained poor and uneducated, the latter part of the Renaissance, according to historian Kieron O'Hara, ushered in "Glimmers of Enlightenment."[12]

Philosophy and the Renaissance

As a forerunner of Enlightenment thinkers, perhaps no one is more important than the French philosopher and mathematician René Descartes, who lived from 1596 to 1650. Descartes believed that all his formal education, with the exception of mathematics, had been worthless. He believed that reason was the only path to true knowledge. He wanted to understand how people could acquire knowledge that is true and absolute, and how one can use reason to prove truth. His philosophical method was to start at the only certain thing that he knew. Writing in the Latin used by all educated people of the time, he stated his one basic certainty: *Cogito ergo sum*. It means, "I think, therefore I am." As O'Hara explains, "Simply by inference from that basic statement, Descartes deduced the existence of the whole world and God with it."[13]

Unlike the philosophers and theologians of his time, Descartes did not want to argue about whether reality existed or whether angels had physical bodies that took up space. Instead, he wanted to prove that humans can logically figure out facts about the world. He attempted to logically demonstrate that God exists and that He created human minds that could correctly understand the world. He said that God would not have created a world that was unreasonable. Descartes believed that the mind and the body are two distinct things. The body is of the physical world, and the mind, or the soul, is of a different nature and can exist without physical reality—after death, for example. The mind controls the body but does not depend on it. To Descartes, reason, not faith, leads people to the goodness of God, and God wants people to use their reason to understand the world.

In 1663 the Church banned Descartes's writings as too radical, but Descartes's ideas were seized upon by others who took them even further. English philosopher Thomas Hobbes, for example, extended the philosophy to argue that the absolute political power of kings was legitimate only if kings used their power for the good of their subjects. Dutch philosopher Baruch de Spinoza, on the other hand, rejected Descartes's idea of mind/body distinction and argued that only the mind, not human physical senses, was real and could understand the world. Further, Spinoza concluded from his thinking that a personal, caring God who makes miracles and has proclaimed laws for humanity does not exist. He said people do not have immortal souls. In 1656 Spinoza's orthodox Jewish community excommunicated him for "monstrous deeds" and "abominable heresies."[14]

No More Status Quo

Dogmatic religious faith and blind submission to absolute political power began to crumble in the Renaissance era despite the resistance of religions and states. In 1517 Martin Luther, a religious philosopher and member of the Catholic clergy, nailed his Ninety-Five Theses to the door of his church in Wittenberg, Germany. The theses condemned Church practices that Luther viewed as corrupt and error-ridden. Thus began the Protestant Reformation. Luther launched a rebellion that eventually led to the Protestant branches of Christianity. Nothing the Catholic Church did could prevent this religious revolution.

Then, in 1688, in mostly Protestant England, fear of the Catholic King James II and his allegiance to the pope resulted in the aristocracy rising up and overthrowing him in favor of his Protestant daughter Mary and her Dutch Protestant husband, William of Orange. As a result of this revolution, the British Parliament of nobles gained supremacy over the monarchy. William and Mary signed a bill of rights that prevented the monarchy from taking certain actions without the consent of Parliament. British monarchs no longer had absolute power.

The Protestant Reformation and the so-called Glorious Revolution of 1688 pushed forward a process that would change Europe's traditional seats of power forever. They planted the seeds that would lead to the explosion of individualism and secularism that marked the Enlightenment era.

Chapter 2

Enlightenment Philosophy and Religion

At its heart the Enlightenment was a philosophical movement. Two men, in large part, were its founders—English mathematician and physicist Isaac Newton and English philosopher John Locke. From this beginning other philosophers and thinkers built a view of humanity and the world that they believed could transform society and civilization. Traditional religion and long-established social norms no longer defined knowledge, morality, or the affairs of humankind.

Newton's Formative Science

In 1687 Isaac Newton published *Principia Mathematica*, the most important physics book ever written. Because of this work, modern-day professor Robert A. Hatch says, Newton is "generally regarded as the most original and influential theorist in the history of science."[15] Newton writes about science, or natural philosophy, as it was called then, but his scientific discoveries had an enormous effect on both philosophy and religion during the Enlightenment. Newton studied the theories of planetary motion developed by Renaissance scientists. He studied Copernicus's theory that the planets orbit the sun, as well as supporting evidence provided by later scientists.

Copernicus's theory had assumed that planets orbited the sun in perfect circles and had offered no explanation as to what kept the planets in place and orbiting. The later Renaissance scientist Johannes Kepler proved mathematically that planetary orbits were elliptical, not circular. He also attempted to develop explanations or laws about the movements of objects, including planets. The astronomer Galileo Galilei was one of the first scientists to use a telescope to view the planets and to observe that Copernicus's explanation of a heliocentric planetary system was true. In addition, Galileo discovered sunspots, proving that the sun was not the perfect body created by God that the Church insisted it was. The moon was not perfect either; it had craters and mountains. Jupiter had moons that revolved around it. So even when it came to moons, Earth was neither special nor the center of God's creation.

Building on the works of these scientists and others and with deep thinking and analysis, Newton developed the law of universal gravitation and his famous three laws of motion. With these laws he transformed science forever. Newton explained with his theory of gravity what Copernicus could not. He demonstrated that all objects attract each other with a universal force of gravitational attraction that depends on the masses of the objects and their distance from each other. When he was an old man, looking back on his great insight, Newton described to his biographer William Stukeley how he thought out his theory of gravity in 1666. Stukeley tells the story of their 1726 interview this way:

> After dinner, the weather being warm, we went into the garden & drank thea [tea] under the shade of some apple tree; only he [Newton] & myself.
>
> Amid other discourse, he told me, he was just in the same situation, as when formerly the notion of gravitation came into his mind. Why sh[oul]d that apple always descend perpendicularly to the ground, thought he to himself; occasion'd by the fall of an apple, as he sat in contemplative mood.
>
> Why sh[oul]d it not go sideways, or upwards? But constantly to the Earth's centre? Assuredly the reason is that the Earth draws it. There must be a drawing power in matter. And the sum of the drawing power in the matter of the Earth must be in the Earth's centre, not in any side of the Earth.

Therefore does this apple fall perpendicularly or towards the centre? If matter thus draws matter; it must be proportion of its quantity. Therefore the apple draws the Earth, as well as the Earth draws the apple.[16]

Newton also told one of his in-laws that his theory expanded as he thought about the force of gravity. This man, John Conduitt, reported, "Why not as high as the Moon said he [Newton] to himself & if so, that must influence her motion & perhaps retain her orbit, whereupon he fell a calculating what would be the effect of that supposition."[17] With his laws, Newton was able to explain the motions of the planets, the moons, comets, and even the ocean tides. With his three laws of motion, Newton explained all movement and how gravity works on everything. The first law is the law of inertia. It states that objects at rest stay at rest and objects in motion stay in motion in the same direction and speed unless acted on by an outside force. The second law is about acceleration and is expressed as a simple math formula: F (force) = m (mass) a (acceleration). Basically, it means that the more force is applied to an object, the more the acceleration, depending on the mass of the object; the smaller the mass, the greater is the effect of the force. The third law states that for every action (or force) there is an equal and opposite reaction (or force). Newton's work demonstrated that the natural world follows natural law. Hatch says, "In sum, Newton's universe united heaven and earth with a single set of laws. It became the physical and intellectual foundation of the modern world view."[18]

From the Supernatural to the Natural

Suddenly, the universe made sense. People did not need God's intervention or miracles to explain the world. Newton said that God had set the universe in motion, but He was not needed to keep it in motion. The universe followed laws that were predictable and understandable. Newton died in 1727, one of the most admired and respected men of his time. The poet Alexander Pope expressed the feelings of many when he wrote at Newton's death, "Nature, and Nature's

English mathematician and physicist Isaac Newton investigates the nature of light. His work with gravity and motion forever transformed science.

Laws lay hid in Night: God said, Let Newton be! and All was Light."[19]

Newton had not only explained natural law, he also demonstrated that by using reason and experience, human beings could understand and master nature. Newton's science had a profound influence on Enlightenment philosophy. Philosophers no longer had to believe that a supernatural power organized and drove the universe. Kieron O'Hara explains, "Natural events needed no rationalization in terms of God's

Skeptic, Fideist, or Atheist?

The Swiss Protestant Pierre Bayle was one of the earliest and most influential of the Enlightenment philosophers. In 1697 he published his great work *The Historical and Critical Dictionary*. In this book Bayle critically and skeptically attacked all religion and moral philosophy that had existed from ancient times to his time. Whether addressing the goodness of God or the existence of evil or the truth of religious tradition, Bayle used his reason to prove that all religion and morality was illogical and contradictory. He argued that only atheism was rationally defensible.

Bayle said, however, that he was not an atheist and maintained his stance as a Protestant Calvinist. He claimed that fideism—the ancient philosophy that morality and religion are based on faith, not reason—was justifiable. Morals and faith in God, he said, do not depend on reason and do not need reason. They are based on emotion and a part of human nature. Religion does not have to be reasonable and ought to be taken on faith. Morality is based on passions and conscience and can be different for different people. Even atheism, he said, is no more than a kind of faith, based on human passion. Because there is no rational basis to believe anything, Bayle argued for complete tolerance of every individual's moral and religious views. His belief in tolerance greatly influenced John Locke, and his reasoning and skepticism influenced the writings of Voltaire and Immanuel Kant.

purpose—they could be explained totally in terms of their physical conditions. Science could not explain *why* things are as they are, but it could explain *how*."[20] This approach to physical laws and the world suggested that many other areas of life could be understood and mastered through the use of reason.

John Locke and the Natural Laws of the Mind

The philosopher and physician John Locke, who lived from 1632 to 1704, was the second major founder of the Enlightenment. Like Newton, who was his friend, he advocated empiricism (using observation and experience) to understand the world, particularly the human mind. Psychology professor Keith Millis and his historical research team explain, "Newton's reductionism and corpuscular view of the world had a direct impact on Locke's theory of the mind. Newton believed the world is composed of basic particles, which he called corpuscles. The force of gravity held these corpuscles together. Likewise, Locke saw the mind as made up of basic constituents. Simple ideas are the basic components. The force of association combines simple ideas to form complex ideas. Locke was the first person to posit this Newtonian-influenced theory of the mind."[21]

Locke wanted to understand how people know things, how they can be sure that their knowledge is true, and how that truth affects the social institutions under which they live. Locke had studied Rene Descartes's theories of the mind, which include the belief that human minds have innate, or inborn, ideas—that they are aware, for example, of the eternal truth that something cannot come from nothing or that God exists. Locke rejected this conclusion. He argued that each person's mind at birth was a *tabula rasa*—a blank slate. Locke explains, "Let us then suppose the mind to be, as we say, white paper, void of all characters, without any ideas; how comes it to be furnished? Whence comes it by that vast store, which the busy and boundless fancy of man has painted on it, with an almost endless variety? Whence has it all the materials of reason and knowledge? To this I answer, in one word, From experience."[22]

Locke believed that every child was born innocent and ready to learn from its environment. This contradicted the Church's teaching that people are born with original sin on their souls because of Adam and Eve's disobedience to God in the Garden of Eden. Children, Locke says, are not born with evil or sinful inclinations that have to be trained or beaten out of them. Instead, children are reasonable beings who develop as they do because of their experiences and their education, beginning with their parents. Children are born with natural tendencies, such as curiosity and a love of freedom, and minds open to guidance. Locke says that children should be taught using reason and that they thus learn to be reasoning people themselves. When brought up rationally and properly educated, people become moral, reasonable, and able to make their own choices.

Locke's Significance and the *Philosophes*

Locke's *tabula rasa* had far-reaching implications for Enlightenment thinkers. It was particularly important for the French intellectuals who came to be known as the *philosophes*. "*Philosophe*" means "philosopher," but the cultural movement of the *philosophes* included all literary people, scientists, philosophers, and thinkers who believed that human reason and empiricism were supreme. The *philosophe* movement, although begun in France, rapidly spread throughout Europe and into the New World. The *philosophe* Claude Adrien Helvetius, for example, followed Locke's theory to its logical conclusion. He spoke for many in the movement when he pointed out that if each person were born a blank slate, then people were born equal. Only the experiences they had as they grew up explained the differences between them. This meant that the difference between ignorant or stupid people and geniuses was only a matter of education. It meant that aristocratic breeding was meaningless. Kings had no divine right to rule, and God had not chosen them as superior to others. The lord of the manor was no more important than the serf. Only good or poor education and the accident of birth distinguished them. Helvetius said, "All men have an equal disposition for understanding."[23]

The idea that people are equal and have an equal ability to use reason to make decisions had another major effect on enlightened thinking. It led to the belief that each individual's desire to pursue happiness was legitimate and natural. O'Hara says that Enlightenment thinkers tried to think of happiness as analogous to Newton's gravity. It was the basis on which humans were moved to use their reason and to lead fulfilled lives. Swiss *philosophe* Jean-Jacques Rousseau explains in his *Discourse*

In Defense of Deism

American founding father Thomas Paine believed that God is the creator but does not intervene in the universe or in human affairs. Paine explains his Deist views:

"There is a happiness in Deism, when rightly understood, that is not to be found in any other system of religion. All other systems have something in them that either shock our reason, or are repugnant to it, and man, if he thinks at all, must stifle his reason in order to force himself to believe them.

But in Deism our reason and our belief become happily united. The wonderful structure of the universe, and everything we behold in the system of the creation, prove to us, far better than books can do, the existence of a God, and at the same time proclaim His attributes.

It is by the exercise of our reason that we are enabled to contemplate God in His works, and imitate Him in His ways. When we see His care and goodness extended over all His creatures, it teaches us our duty toward each other, while it calls forth our gratitude to Him. It is by forgetting God in His works, and running after the books of pretended revelation, that man has wandered from the straight path of duty and happiness, and become by turns the victim of doubt and the dupe of delusion."

Thomas Paine, "Of the Religion of Deism Compared with the Christian Religion," reprinted in Paul Halsall, Internet Modern History Sourcebook, Fordham University, 1998. www.fordham.edu.

on Inequality that "self-love is a natural sentiment which prompts every animal to watch over its own conservation and which, directed in man by reason and modified by pity [sympathy and empathy for others] produces humanity and virtue."[24] Therefore, every individual in society has the right to the pursuit of happiness, including the happiness of thinking for oneself.

New Attitudes About Religion

If all people are equal, then it logically follows, say both Locke and the *philosophes*, that tolerance for one another's views is necessary. Enlightened thinkers rejected, for example, the idea of one true religion. Locke once lamented, "It is not the diversity of opinions (which cannot be avoided), but the refusal of toleration to those that are of different opinions . . . , that has produced all the bustles and wars that have been in the Christian world upon account of religion."[25] Enlightenment theory held that each person uses his or her own reason to make decisions about morality or religion or other beliefs. Each person's beliefs are of equal value. No one can claim superiority or the right to power over others—not even religious leaders.

The leading Enlightenment *philosophe*, Voltaire (real name Francois-Marie Arouet), was a writer and historian to whom religious tolerance and freedom were of major importance. Voltaire interpreted history in terms of the human mind and the resulting progress of civilization. With his studies of history he wanted to show that concepts of morality were a part of the natural laws that governed humanity and that as human reason progressed culture and society in turn improved and progressed. In direct contradiction to Renaissance thinkers, he believed that his modern era was superior to that of ancient Rome or Greece because scientific ideas were gradually replacing religious ideas. The world would be bettered in the future as reasonable minds continued to overcome religious mysticism and ignorance.

Voltaire rejected all organized religion as superstitious and intolerant. He was especially angry at Christianity in the form of the Catholic Church. Voltaire thought the powerful Church used its teachings and dogma to control people and their minds, interfering with the development of reason and educated thought. He once wrote, "The superstitious man is to the rogue what the slave is to the tyrant. Further, the superstitious man is governed by the fanatic and becomes fanatic. Superstition born in Paganism, adopted by Judaism, infested the Christian Church from the earliest times. All the fathers of the Church, without exception, believed in the power of magic. The Church always condemned magic, but she always believed in it: she did not excommunicate sorcerers as madmen who were mistaken, but as men who were really in communication with the devil."[26]

Voltaire, the leading Enlightenment philosophe, *believed that human reason and knowledge would overcome ignorance. In his view, organized religion only fostered superstition and intolerance.*

Reason Is the New Morality

The *philosophes* as a whole believed that their thinking about humanity and society could transform the world. They would use the scientific method to understand people, educate and guide people, and usher in a new and better civilization. Historian Steven Kreis explains, "The new science was the science of man."[27] With their stress on the individual, tolerance, and natural laws, many of them rejected organized religion because of its reliance on faith, and they strongly opposed state-supported religion of any kind. They used philosophy to determine what morality was, and they searched for a social or political system that could be based on natural law. They were united in their belief in individual freedom of thought and in individual inalienable rights, including freedom of religion.

The great German philosopher Immanuel Kant believed that most people were fearful of challenging traditions and religious dogma and thinking for themselves. In 1784 he wrote an essay titled "What Is Enlightenment?" He argued that enlightenment was intellectual freedom. He said that he did not yet live in an enlightened age in which all people were liberated from authority, but it was nonetheless an age of enlightenment. Kant famously urged humanity, "Dare to know!"[28]

A Different Approach to God

Even though they criticized Christianity as an organized religion, however, most Enlightenment thinkers were not antireligion. They were extremely skeptical about miracles, God punishing people with disease or disaster, or any kind of divine intervention that interfered mysteriously with natural laws. They did not want to take any religious teachings on faith. Instead, even very devout Enlightenment thinkers based their religion on reason. Newton and Locke were both convinced of the existence of God. Newton believed that all the order, beauty, and perfection of natural laws proved that God—a supreme intelligence—had created and designed the universe. Perhaps God also intervened to keep all the laws of motion working so flawlessly. Locke simply argued that without God, no one's existence made any sense.

To Enlightenment thinkers God was, above all, reasonable. He did not violate His own laws of nature. The way the world worked was logical, and God had given people the capacity to reason it out. Samuel Clarke, a priest of the Church of England, for example, argued that Jesus's teachings were obviously right to any reasonable person. Clarke supports Jesus's Golden Rule, for instance, by saying, "Whatever I judge reasonable or unreasonable, that another should do for me, that by the same judgment I declare reasonable or unreasonable, that I in the like case should do for him. . . . That which is good is fit and reasonable, and that which is evil is unreasonable to be done."[29] Christian doctrine, therefore, is supported by Enlightenment thinking, and morality can be achieved by reason. Enlightenment thinkers might argue about whether Jesus walked on water or was resurrected from the dead or whether the entire Bible was literally true, but they could still believe in God and Jesus's teachings. And they still advocated tolerance for others' beliefs.

Deism

Many Enlightenment thinkers, such as Clarke, remained faithful to an organized religion on the basis of their reason, but many others rejected the idea of a particular church's dogma and became Deists. Deism is the belief in God as the creator but who does not intervene in the universe or in the affairs of humankind in a miraculous way. It is based only upon rational thinking, and it rejects the idea of divine revelation. That is, Deists generally do not believe that God reveals truths to prophets who then teach people God's holy laws. Enlightenment Deists saw their individual reason as a gift from God that could be used to understand Him. In Europe during the eighteenth century Immanuel Kant, Jean-Jacques Rousseau, and Voltaire were among the leading Deists.

In the New World, Enlightenment Deism had a profound influence. Some Deists in America were Ethan Allen, Benjamin Franklin, Thomas Paine, Thomas Jefferson, and probably George Washington and James Madison. Jefferson studied the European Deists and was a Christian Deist. History professor Peter S. Onuf says of Jefferson,

"For this apostle of reason, the natural world was like a great book, made legible to scientists (or 'natural philosophers') through its predictable and lawful patterns. Enlightened men who discerned nature's laws could begin to master the world, promoting the improvement of man's lot and fulfilling God's original intentions for His creation. Even politics could be reduced to a science."[30]

Jefferson was a follower of Jesus because of the pure goodness of his teachings and his efforts to reform his society. Jefferson believed that the ethical system that Jesus brought to the world was the best ever conceived, saying that Christianity is the "religion of all others most friendly to liberty, science, and the freest expansion of the human mind."[31] He thought organized religion had distorted and tainted Jesus's teachings with mysticism and miracles and traditional church rituals. He carefully studied the Bible so as to determine exactly what Jesus had said, as opposed to what others claimed about him. He thought that many of the Gospels had been corrupted by mysticism and were in error. So, for the private use of himself and his family, Jefferson devoted himself to extracting Jesus's teachings from the New Testament. He wrote his own version—now known as the Jefferson Bible—removing all the supernatural and miraculous stories and keeping only Jesus's words and ethical teachings. To Jefferson, this rational, common sense approach to Christianity was the best way to understand the scriptures and God. He once wrote to his nephew, "Your own reason is the only oracle given you by heaven."[32]

A Unity of Religion and Natural Law

For Enlightenment thinkers and leaders, religion was not in contradiction to philosophy or science but a devoutly rational way to understand the universe and God. And their religion was a path toward creating a more perfect human condition.

Chapter 3

Enlightenment Arts and Science

The basic tenets of Enlightenment philosophy were meaningful in almost all aspects of European and American culture. The belief that happiness was a virtue, for example, influenced Enlightenment art. Individualism and the ideal of human equality influenced poetry, literature, and music. The supremacy of reason and the decline in dependency on religious dogma aided the development of the sciences. Optimistic, enlightened people believed that reason and the knowledge of natural laws would improve their civilization and culture without limit and in every facet of life.

Early Enlightenment Art

To enlightened artists, happiness and aesthetic appreciation of nature were based on reason and thus should be celebrated by society. Increasing one's happiness was natural and virtuous, and so, during the first half of the Enlightenment era, beauty for beauty's sake was justified and acceptable in art. Artistic style during the first half of the eighteenth century represented a rejection of the formality of the Baroque style of the seventeenth century.

During the Baroque era of the 1600s, artists in painting, sculpture, and architecture had already moved away from the strictly religious subject matter of the medieval period and entered a new period of both secular and religious art that emphasized creativity and beauty. Baroque art was grandeur and drama. This sophisticated artwork of the Renaissance honored both the glory of God and the beauty and glory of ideal humanity, in accordance with the humanistic philosophy of the era. It was art with a purpose, especially meant to be dramatic and to invoke serious emotions in the viewer, such as awe, grief, majestic spirituality, love, ecstasy, and pity.

In the early part of the Enlightenment, artists came to see Baroque art as too pompous, pretentious, and serious. Instead, early Enlightenment artists developed the style known as rococo. Rococo artists rejected uplifting and impressive artworks in favor of enjoyable, lighthearted playfulness. They embraced beauty for its own sake and decoration for the fun of it. Artists generally avoided meaningful art that portrayed holy themes or heroic figures and instead depicted happy, carefree subject matter. They celebrated the beauty of nature with patterns, colors, and curves based on flowers, vines, and shells. French painter Jean-Antoine Watteau was the father of the rococo style. He often created elaborate, colorful landscapes and gardens that were peopled by beautifully costumed aristocratic human figures at leisure or in romantic poses. His most famous oil painting, named variously *Pilgrimage to the Island of Cythera* or *Embarkation for Cythera*, depicts a mythical island of romance where lovers go to find their partners.

The rococo style of lavish, lush ornamentation quickly spread throughout Europe and became popular with the middle class and aristocracy alike. People not only admired and acquired rococo paintings but also decorated their homes with small ceramic pieces, furniture, and fancy silver serving pieces for their dinner tables. Each piece was heavily adorned with decorations such as flowers and leaves, plump cherubs, curving lines, gilding, and pastel colors.

Neoclassical Art

Eventually, the heavily ornamented rococo style came to be seen as too frivolous, with too much decoration. Enlightenment taste became more serious. Artists became more interested in depicting the truths to be found in nature and the capabilities of humanity than in playful decorations and fantasy. They wanted, instead, to depict enlightened, educational themes. By the 1780s neoclassical art was developed, partly

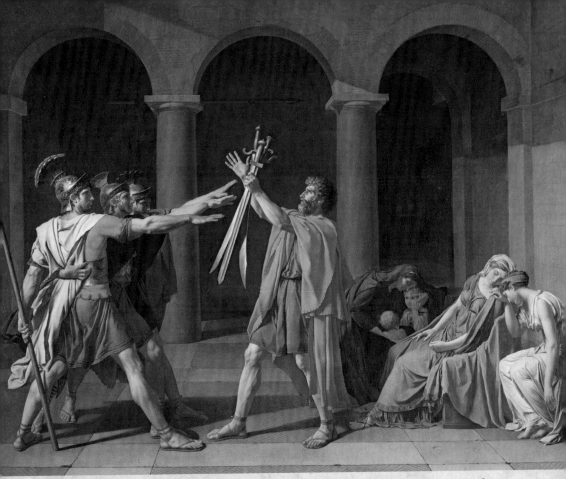

Jacques-Louis David's The Oath of the Horatii *(pictured) is an example of the neoclassical style of painting. The painting depicts self-sacrifice for a noble cause, reflecting the Enlightenment's emphasis on reasoned morality.*

in reaction to archeological discoveries of ancient Greek and Roman ruins. Artists were impressed by the elegant lines of Greek and Roman civilization's architecture and sculptures. They sought to express the dignity of humans and the reasoned morality of the Enlightenment in a beautiful, classical style.

French artist Jacques-Louis David's 1784 painting *The Oath of the Horatii* is a famous example of the neoclassical style. The painting depicts three brothers pledging their lives to the defense of Rome in obedience to their father. The painting is heroic and patriotic and represents virtuous self-sacrifice to a noble cause—the reasoned morality of the Enlightenment presented in a classical scene. The American painter Benjamin West used the neoclassical style to celebrate the reason and capability of an enlightened man: Benjamin Franklin. Franklin is painted in the midst of a dark thunderstorm, flying his kite with a key attached to the string. A spark of lightning is jumping from the key to his knuckle, proving for the first time that lightning is a form of electricity. The painting—while depicting a disputed and perhaps legendary event—is an expression of the Enlightenment theme of man's mastery of nature.

Music

Painting was not the only art genre to which Enlightenment themes brought creativity. Kieron O'Hara says, for instance, "The progress of music was a triumph of the Enlightenment period."[33] Wolfgang Amadeus Mozart is perhaps the embodiment of Enlightenment musical genius. The musical talent was Mozart's own, but especially in his operas he expressed Enlightenment themes. In *The Marriage of Figaro*, for example, the aristocrats are portrayed as immoral, ignoble people, no better than anyone else. Figaro is a servant, but he is a free man and demands the right to make his own choices. In *The Magic Flute* a trio of messengers echoes the Enlightenment themes of reason and rejection of religious mysticism. They sing, "Superstition will die, soon the wise will prevail."[34]

Literature

Eighteenth-century novels, too, reflected Enlightenment philosophy and values. During this time a new kind of fiction appeared that focused on one individual and his or her experiences. The author often tried to show how the individual was a product of society or how the protagonist was affected psychologically by the plot experiences. Daniel Defoe, for instance, wrote *Robinson Crusoe* in the form of a diary that seemed so authentic that some uneducated people believed that it was true. Crusoe—who survives a shipwreck and is marooned on an island—is not a heroic, noble, or mystical figure but simply an ordinary man coping with extraordinary circumstances and learning to adjust to his experiences. His emotional

Enlightenment Poetry

Enlightenment poets expressed the era's ideals of rationality and the equality of individuals in their works. Alexander Pope, who lived from 1688 to 1744, was an admired English poet. His poem *An Essay on Man* was written in 1734. Epistle 2 of the long poem famously opens, "Know, then, thyself, presume not God to scan; The proper study of mankind is man." Pope believed that the universe follows a divine plan, but people can never understand God or His plan and should not even try. Instead, people should use their reason to understand humanity and the natural laws that govern life.

The greatest poet of the Enlightenment era was Robert Burns, who wrote in the Scottish dialect. Although sometimes difficult for modern readers to understand, the common dialect was a way to express democratic ideals and the worth of the lower-class person. His poem *A Man's a Man for A' That*, written in 1795, is a call for democracy and social justice. The last stanza is:

Then let us pray that come it may,
(As come it will for a' that,)
That Sense and Worth, o'er a' the earth,
Shall bear the gree, an' a' that.
For a' that, an' a' that,
It's coming yet for a' that,
That Man to Man, the world o'er,
Shall brothers be for a' that.

(In the poem, "a" means "all"; "bear the gree" means "take the prize"; "It's coming yet" means that democracy will win in the end.)

Alexander Pope, *Essay on Man*, Project Gutenberg eBook, August 20, 2007. www.gutenberg.org.

Robert Burns, *A Man's a Man for A' That*, Burns Country, Robert Burns.org. www.robertburns.org.

and psychological reactions are the most important part of the story.

In another of Defoe's great novels, *Moll Flanders*, the independent individual is a woman who spurns a woman's traditional role in society. Moll Flanders is an unimportant member of London's poorest class who is self-reliant, strong, and determined to pursue the happiness of wealth and status in her own way. She defies all convention and social standards, is the equal of any man, goes through many dramatic experiences, and eventually finds prosperity in her old age.

Voltaire used satire and wit to express Enlightenment values in his writings—and also, with enlightened skepticism, to make fun of Enlightenment optimism and philosophy. In his 1759 novel *Candide*, Voltaire bitterly attacks almost every social institution by exaggeratedly describing the awful misery caused by religion, the monarchy, the aristocracy, and even the optimism and trust in the reasonable God of the *philosophes*. The book is a tirade against the injustice of church and state, but it also laughs at philosophers for believing they understand everything and failing to fight injustice in the real world. Dr. Pangloss, a ridiculous, optimistic academic in the story believes in "metaphysico-theologo-cosmolo-nigology."[35] The made-up word is Voltaire's way of ridiculing fashionable philosophy. In the face of any horrible disaster Pangloss does nothing but talk and philosophize. When Candide is dying of thirst, for example, Pangloss gives him a speech instead of some water. Pangloss represents all that angered Voltaire about the Enlightenment leaders and their failure to address real-world iniquities and inequalities. He strongly believed in equality, fairness, and individual rights. He argued in his writings that science and reason should be used to prevent and mitigate unnecessary suffering in the world.

Most Enlightenment literature had an underlying educational purpose. The writers were describing and analyzing society and the individual's place within it. Literature had a wide and receptive audience during the eighteenth century, and novels, poetry, and nonfiction had a meaningful effect on general social attitudes. Many literate and educated people existed in all classes of society by the time of the Enlightenment era. Books were readily available, and people hungered for them, both for entertainment and for knowledge.

Diderot's *Encyclopédie*

Between 1751 and 1772 two leading *philosophes*—Denis Diderot and Jean le Rond d'Alembert—published a massive encyclopedia with the goal of creating a complete compilation of all human knowledge. Altogether, 140 different Enlightenment authors wrote 71,818 articles for the *Encyclopédie*, as it is known in French. Diderot and d'Alembert wrote thousands themselves. D'Alembert concentrated mostly on science and math articles, while Diderot wrote about subjects as diverse as how to make jam, how the clothing industry functioned, and what an encyclopedia is. The *Encyclopédie* also covered topics such as religion, politics, and philosophy. Among the contributors were Voltaire and Jean-Jacques Rousseau.

The goal of the encyclopedia was to make knowledge about everything available to everyone. In accordance with Enlightenment values, every topic in the *Encyclopédie* was examined critically, skeptically, and analytically. Diderot said it was the duty of enlightened thinkers to spread the Enlightenment everywhere. As the chief editor in charge of the *Encyclopédie*, he believed he was working for the good of all people, spreading knowledge and helping to wipe out superstition. In his article defining the encyclopedia, he says, "This is a work that cannot be completed except by a society of men of letters and skilled workmen, each working separately on his own part, but all bound together solely by their zeal for the best interests of the human race and a feeling of mutual good will."[36]

The publication of the first seven volumes of the *Encyclopédie* created a furor in France. At that time, all published books had to be approved by the king's censors. They refused to sanction the controversial *Encyclopédie* with its Enlightenment philosophy, discourses about individual rights, scientific and logical questioning of Church dogma, philosophical discussions of natural laws, and moral criticisms of French politics. Notably, the *Encyclopédie* listed religion as merely one philosophy among many. The Catholic Church was outraged by this perceived attack. In order to placate the Church, King Louis XV banned the *Encyclopédie*—although he never enforced the ban. D'Alembert

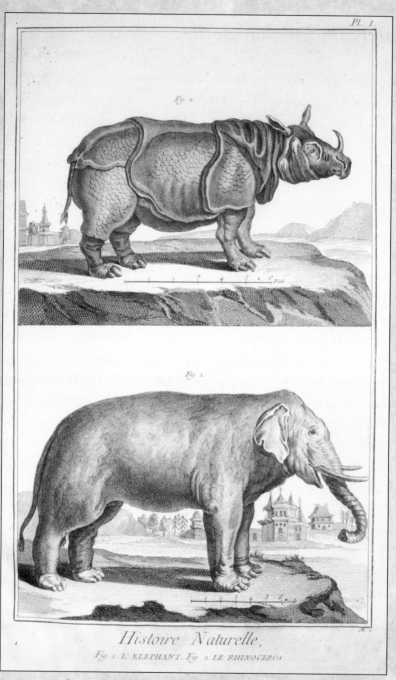

Histoire Naturelle,
Fig. 1. L'ELEPHANT. Fig. 2. LE RHINOCEROS

An engraving from the Encyclopédie *published by Denis Diderot and Jean le Rond d'Alembert accurately depicts a rhinoceros and an elephant. The idea behind the massive work was to make knowledge on any number of subjects available to anyone who wished to learn.*

eventually dropped out of the project, but Diderot continued it until all thirty-two volumes were completed. In the end, the *Encyclopédie* had a major effect on the politics, religion, and education of millions of people throughout France and Europe. It challenged the authority of the Church and government and, some historians say, helped to inspire both the American and French Revolutions.

Enlightenment Science

As enlightened thinking and knowledge about natural laws spread, the influence of religion declined and that of science advanced. No major scientific breakthroughs occurred during the eighteenth century, but steady progress was made in exploring the natural world and explaining natural phenomena that had previously been understood to be supernatural or miraculous in origin.

On Sunday, November 1, 1755, the religious holiday of All Saints Day, a strong earthquake followed by a large tsunami and then major fires destroyed the city of Lisbon, Portugal. Modern scientists estimate the earthquake's magnitude as between 8.7 and 9 on the Richter scale. Thousands died as they worshipped in churches. Thousands more died in their homes, in the tsunami, and in the fires. Historians believe that as many as half of the city's one hundred thousand residents were killed.

Many Catholic Church leaders blamed the disaster on the sins of Lisbon's people or the sins of Portugal itself. They declared that the earthquake was an example of God's wrath and His divine justice. This response was the typical interpretation of disasters offered by the Church at the time, but this time, Enlightenment thinkers rose up in outrage over the religious point of view. Nuns and priests were killed; devout worshippers were killed; innocent babies and children were killed. To believe that these people deserved God's punishment was unreasonable and insupportable. Instead, enlightened thinkers searched for a rational, scientific explanation.

No one in the eighteenth century understood the science of earthquakes, but Immanuel Kant, even though he was not a scientist, tried to explain the disaster in terms of natural laws. Modern day philosopher

Martin Schönfeld explains, "Kant speculated that there are giant caves underneath mountain ridges. Sometimes gases in the caves form combustible mixtures. When they blow up, the caves collapse, shaking the earth. . . . Kant insists on secular explanations. Earthquakes are terrible, but they are accidents. We do not know what they mean in the larger frame of things, and to interpret the Lisbon earthquake as a divine punishment is naïve."[37] Kant's explanation was wrong, but it

The Grand Tour

During the eighteenth century, with the rise in wealth, leisure time, and education, it became fashionable for aristocratic and middle-class people alike to travel throughout Europe for several months or years to see significant sites. Especially for wealthy British and American people the Grand Tour was an essential part of their education, but Europeans from all nations participated. The most important places to visit were Italy and France. People went to Italy to see the ancient ruins of Rome. Art students often remained to attend the French Academy in Rome and to learn about Roman architecture. Tourists traveled to Naples to visit the nearby recent archeological digs at Pompeii, Herculaneum, and Paestum. They visited Florence and Venice to admire the classical artworks there and often had their own portraits painted. People visited Paris to learn the latest etiquette and to argue philosophy in the salons of aristocratic women who hosted the French *philosophes* or to debate politics in Parisian coffeehouses. The Grand Tour was an important custom—proof of one's wealth and freedom— for anyone who aspired to cultured intellectual status and high social standing. It also established the popularity of collecting ancient artifacts as souvenirs and acquiring artworks and copies of famous paintings for display in private homes.

represented a major step forward in the search for a reasonable approach to natural disasters.

Science and the Age of Earth

Scientists began to question other religious dogma about Earth as well, especially its age. Christian religious leaders insisted that God had created Earth in 4004 BCE. This date was calculated by Irish Anglican Bishop James Ussher in the middle of the seventeenth century. Ussher spent years carefully studying the Bible and its chronology of events so as to assign dates for the generations of people since Adam and Eve, important biblical occurrences, and the date of the world's creation. He also correlated his dating efforts with some non-Christian sources, such as the dates of the lives of the Babylonian kings listed by the Greek astronomer Ptolemy. In 1701 the Church of England officially adopted Ussher's dates as accurate. Even in that era, however, critics questioned this conclusion on the basis of the evidence in the natural world.

In 1715 Edmund Halley, the astronomer for whom Halley's Comet is named, thought of using the salt in the ocean as a kind of geological clock that would show the age of Earth. Halley observed that streams and rivers were constantly picking up and carrying small amounts of salt into the oceans. So he thought that measuring the density of ocean salt, which would increase over time, could yield an accurate measure of Earth's age. Since he did not know how much salt was in the oceans in the past, Halley could not use his salt clock method, but he proposed measuring salt content over time in the present to learn the rate of increase and using this rate to figure out Earth's age. He never performed this experiment, which would not have worked anyway because a salt clock would be inaccurate, but he did theorize about Earth's age. He said that Earth could not be just a few thousand years old or else the oceans would be mostly freshwater. Neither could it be infinitely old, or else the oceans would all have as much salt as the Dead Sea.

Halley was only guessing about the age of Earth, but he did influence other scientists with his belief that Earth had a history that was older than human history. These scientists also theorized that Earth was much older than Ussher's calculations suggested. In 1770 Abraham Werner, by studying rocks and fossils, proposed that Earth had once been under an ocean and might be a million years old. In 1774 the French mathematician and naturalist Georges-Louis Leclerc, Comte de Buffon, looked to natural laws to determine Earth's age. Buffon guessed that a comet had knocked off pieces of the sun and formed the planets. Then, as Earth gradually cooled life spontaneously formed, and over time many different species developed. Buffon estimated that Earth was about seventy-five thousand years old, since it would take such a time frame for changes in animal species to occur. Buffon was mistaken in all his ideas, but his work was influential in the science of the Enlightenment. The website Understanding Evolution explains, "It may be true that no single idea of Buffon's has withstood the test of time. But his work was still a milestone of science because he thought about the Earth and life in ways that few had before—both life and the Earth had a history."[38]

Exploring the Natural World

In addition to advancing theories about Earth's age, Enlightenment scientists made strides in the areas of biology and other aspects of the natural world. Carl Linnaeus, a Swedish naturalist, developed a classification system for living organisms based on the characteristics and structures they had in common. He grouped them by kingdom, class, order, family, genus, and species—a framework that is still used today. Linnaeus grouped plants on the basis of their reproductive parts—a classification system that has been modified in modern times—and he compared plant reproduction to human love. In 1729 he wrote, "The flowers' leaves . . . serve as bridal beds which the Creator has so gloriously arranged, adorned with such noble bed curtains, and perfumed with so many soft scents that the bridegroom with his bride might there celebrate their nuptials with so much the greater solemnity. When now the bed is so prepared, it is time for the bridegroom to embrace his beloved bride and offer her his gifts."[39]

Today this might sound like a silly, sentimental way to describe

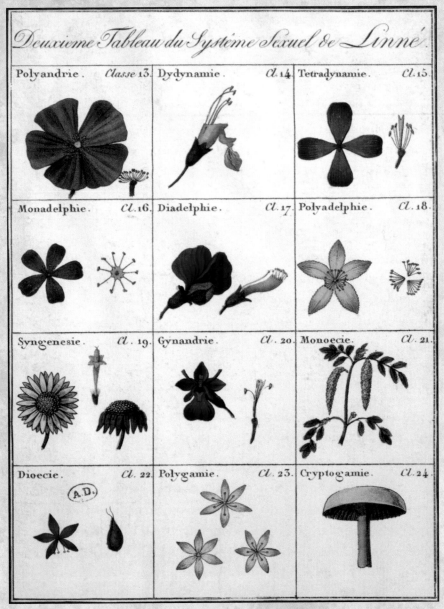

Deuxieme Tableau du Systéme Sexuel de Linné.

Polyandrie. Classe 13.	Dydynamie. Cl. 14.	Tetradynamie. Cl. 15.
Monadelphie. Cl. 16.	Diadelphie. Cl. 17.	Polyadelphie. Cl. 18.
Syngenesie. Cl. 19.	Gynandrie. Cl. 20.	Monoecie. Cl. 21.
Dioecie. Cl. 22.	Polygamie. Cl. 23.	Cryptogamie. Cl. 24.

Swedish naturalist Carl Linnaeus developed a classification system for living organisms based on common structures and characteristics. The Second Table of the Plant Sexual System (pictured) is one of many that appear in Linnaeus's work.

plant stamens and pistils, but in Linnaeus's time, it was controversial and too sexy for many thinkers. One academician, Johann Siegesbeck, was outraged by the description. He called Linnaeus's plant classification "loathsome harlotry"[40] because it assigned sexual activity to God's beautiful plants. Linnaeus got his revenge on his critic, though—he named a particularly small, insignificant, worthless weed after him.

Among other efforts to explain and understand the natural world was Enlightenment research with electricity. In 1745 two scientists independently invented the Leyden jar for storing static electricity. German scientist Ewald Georg von Kleist and Dutch scientist Pieter van Musschenbroek devised this combination of a glass bottle partially filled with water and with a metal wire passing through the cork that stoppered the bottle. Soon other scientists, including Benjamin Franklin, improved upon the design and used Leyden jars to do electrical experiments. Franklin eventually developed a sort of electrical battery by connecting a group of Leyden jars together, and he came up with the theory of positive and negative electricity. He also had fun with his electrical experiments. He roasted a fowl on a spit turned by electricity, made a fake spider move with electricity, and charged glasses of wine so that people got a small shock when they tried to drink the wine.

And Science Becomes Popular

Whether in electricity or life sciences or geological theories, men such as Franklin popularized science during the Enlightenment age. People marveled at and applauded Franklin's electrical demonstrations. They eagerly read popular science books, and in Europe they attended science lectures for entertainment. People flocked to botanical and zoological gardens. The botanical garden in Paris—the Jardin des Plantes—was directed by Buffon, who allowed the public to tour it.

At the beginning of the eighteenth century the books most often bought were theological and religious; by the end of the era, the most frequently purchased books were fiction or popular science. Governments, too, were accepting popular science, at least sometimes, because science seemed to offer a way to control the natural environment in areas such as public health and engineering. After the Lisbon earthquake, Portugal's minister Sebastiao de Carvalho e Melo, Marquis of Pombal, used science to rebuild with earthquake-resistant buildings in the city's center. Historian Dorinda Outram says, "Science was becoming acceptable as a form of knowledge worth pursuing in spite of both the jeers of the unlearned, and the *caveats* [skeptical warnings] of the philosophers. . . . It had begun to offer claims to control, exploit and predict nature and society, to provide secular knowledge, where man's knowledge of the universe could become independent from that of its creator."[41] Enlightenment ideas were permeating societies and changing the thought processes by which even ordinary people understood the world.

Chapter 4

Enlightenment Politics and Revolution

The emphasis on the individual and rationalism, along with skepticism about tradition and traditional authority, inevitably gave rise to political liberalism. Enlightenment political views were defined by a belief in individual freedom, individual rights, and tolerance for others. Liberalism was a demand for rational political systems that emphasized the common good. Enlightenment thinkers debated the very nature of government and its legitimate role in society. They recognized the need for some kind of government, since complete individual freedom is not feasible in any society. However, they subscribed to the view that liberty was a moral imperative, and that meant the freedom to do anything that was not prohibited by enlightened law. What sort of government was best for achieving this end and how the government should function was vigorously debated. For some Enlightenment leaders government reform was appropriate, but for others the only answer was revolution.

The Right to Rule

During the eighteenth century almost all European countries and nation-states were monarchies. In some, particularly England after the Glorious Revolution, kings and queens ruled through the consent of members of the aristocracy, who participated in government themselves, and monarchal authority was constrained by laws. England's political system represented the beginnings of the constitutional monarchy. In other European areas rulers were absolute monarchs—answerable to no one and able to wield power unrestrained by laws or a constitution.

For the most part tradition dictated that monarchs ruled by divine right, meaning the monarchy as a whole and every individual king or queen was chosen by God to have ultimate authority. In this view kings and queens were not ordinary humans. They were rightfully elite and derived their right to power from God and the Church. Church and state were intertwined, since religion supported the ruler's status. The class of nobles and aristocrats had been determined by God, too, as was the class of peasants and serfs.

This belief system changed during the Enlightenment. Even monarchs no longer believed in the religious right to absolute power. Nevertheless, even though their authority became more secular, they believed that the strong centralized government of their monarchies was necessary for the good of the state and its people.

Absolute Monarchy

Some Enlightenment thinkers believed that the best form of government was an absolute but enlightened monarchy. Voltaire, for example, argued that a good, enlightened monarch—advised by enlightened philosophers—would be able to promote reason and science and end superstition, ignorance, and intolerance. The monarch would have the responsibility to enlighten the country's citizens and promote a modern civilization for the good of the people. He or she would support individual liberty, allow freedom of speech, prevent religious persecution, and educate the nation's youth in reason.

Voltaire wanted the monarch's power to be absolute because he did not want the Church or the aristocracy to be able to stand in the way of change. Catholicism was the state religion of France, and Voltaire thought that its clergy promoted tradition and intolerance. He viewed the French aristocracy—who formed the high courts of France—as enforcing laws only to benefit themselves. These high courts were called *Parlements*.

Catherine the Great of Russia, depicted on horseback in royal riding regalia, tried to modernize her country. She instituted agricultural and industrial reforms and expanded education for the noble and middle classes.

The French aristocracy truly was often self-serving, oppressive, and cruel. Through the *Parlements* the aristocracy interfered with efforts to fight injustice instead of ruling on laws and cases fairly and rationally. In 1748, for example, King Louis XV tried to impose an income tax that applied to every individual of every social class. The *Parlements* were angry because the clergy and nobility were traditionally exempt from taxes, and they forced the king to rescind the tax. *Parlements* also authorized torture for criminals, which the king was unable to stop. Louis XV was a weak and unenlightened king, but Voltaire believed that an enlightened despot could break the power of the aristocratic class and the Church and bring liberty, equality, and the benefits of enlightened thinking to the people.

Enlightened Monarchs

Some European monarchs were heavily influenced by Enlightenment ideals and tried to rule as enlightened despots. Their principle of government was, as Austria's emperor Joseph II said, "Everything for the people, nothing by the people."[42] Joseph ruled Austria as an absolute monarch for ten years—from 1780 to his death in 1790. During that time he made many reforms, including abolishing the feudal practice of serfdom, instituting freedom of the press, setting up a system of secular schools, and guaranteeing freedom of religion.

Another enlightened monarch of the era was Catherine the Great of Russia, who ruled for thirty years after her ascent to the throne in 1762. She tried to modernize Russia by instituting agricultural and industrial reforms and supporting foreign investments to aid the Russian economy. She also pushed for education for the noble and middle classes. Voltaire was a great admirer of Catherine as an enlightened monarch. He never met her, but he maintained a correspondence with her and praised her for "civilizing" Russia and turning it into an economic success story. Once, before embarking on a difficult trip, he wrote to her, "If I should die on the road, I will put on my little tomb: Here lies the admirer of the august Catherine."[43]

But Catherine the Great was not a perfectly enlightened monarch. By other accounts she was haughty, stubborn, and extremely authoritarian. She did nothing to eliminate serfdom from Russia, where the majority of the people—the peasants—lived in near slavery. The same was true of another enlightened monarch, Frederick the Great of Prussia. While complaining about the plight of the serfs, Frederick did nothing to change the feudal system. He once explained that to abolish serfdom "would entirely overthrow the mode of managing estates [of the nobility]"[44] and would cause financial loss and suffering for the aristocrats.

Enlightened monarchs did not always benefit their people, and most monarchs in Europe were not interested in Enlightenment ideals

Adam Smith, Father of Modern Capitalism

Adam Smith was a Scottish Enlightenment philosopher and political economist. In 1776 he published his influential book *An Inquiry into the Nature and Causes of the Wealth of Nations*, in which he advocated enlightened self-interest as the most ethical economic system. In his book Smith explains his theories of how societies function and acquire wealth and which economic system results in the most good for the most people. In Smith's time nations practiced protectionism. The rulers believed that exporting goods to increase the gold and silver in the treasury was desirable, but imports were heavily regulated and taxed to prevent money from leaving the country.

Smith, by contrast, believed in the value of free trade, in which the "invisible hand" of an unregulated system controls supply and demand to the benefit of all. He reasoned that the common good is best served by the individual freedom to sell one's labor and goods, and that true wealth should be measured not in money but in labor and production. He explained that freedom and enlightened self-interest was a better system than having kings and governments control the economy. He argued that economic and social freedom would help the poor become prosperous, while protectionism, monopolies, and laws to protect workers, such as bans on labor-saving devices that might result in fewer workers being hired, ended up keeping them poor. The free market and working in one's own self-interest are forces for good and help everyone achieve a better life. Today, Smith is often called the father of modern capitalism.

anyway. Many enlightened thinkers vigorously disagreed with those like Voltaire who believed in the merits of absolute monarchies. Some argued that constitutional monarchies were preferable because they guaranteed a check on the powers of a single individual. Voltaire's contemporary Charles-Louis de Secondat, Baron de La Brède et de Montesquieu admired the British form of government. It had three branches of government—the executive (the monarch), the legislature (Parliament), and the judiciary—and although not really separate, each branch effectively limited the power of the others. Montesquieu thought that this system was the best way to guarantee liberty to the people. Others, like the Enlightenment playwright Franz Kratter, opposed the very idea that a despot could be anything but cruel and oppressive. He once said, "Absolute monarchies are but one step away from despotism. Despotism and Enlightenment: let anyone who can try to reconcile these two. I can't."[45]

The Consent of the Governed

Despite the limited freedoms associated with a monarchal system of government, many Enlightenment leaders were opposed to the idea of a democratic or republican form of government. Montesquieu thought a republic would be impractical because the will of the majority could so easily limit liberty for all, and nothing would stand in the way of majority decisions; there would be no checks and balances. Many others feared that the unenlightened, uneducated masses were simply incapable of governing themselves and that a republic or democracy would soon degenerate into chaos or mob rule.

Nevertheless, some Enlightenment leaders were strongly influenced by John Locke's ideas about government, freedom, and the natural rights of every individual. Locke says, "Men being, as has been said, by nature, all free, equal, and independent, no one can be put out of this estate, and subjected to the political power of another, without his own consent. The only way whereby any one divests himself of his natural liberty, and puts on the bonds of civil society, is by agreeing with other men to join and unite into a community for their comfortable, safe, and peaceable living one amongst another, in a secure enjoyment of their properties, and a greater security against any, that are not of it."[46]

Enlightenment and the American Revolution

Locke did not specify the form of government that would ensure it operates only with the consent of the governed, but in America, other enlightened thinkers did. Many historians say that Locke is the philosophical father of the United States of America. Thomas Jefferson, for instance, believed passionately in the ideals expounded by Locke. In 1774 Jefferson wrote an essay in which he accused King George III of violating the pact with the governed that all monarchs should honor. Jefferson wrote that by interfering with the political decisions of the colony of Virginia, the king was exercising an unlawful authority. In America the king did not have the consent of the governed, and the subjects of England had rights that were being denied to the subjects of Virginia.

Jefferson was but one of the many enlightened leaders of American politics who objected to the king's use of authority while ignoring the colonies' rights to representation in the decision-making process. The legislatures of the separate colonies formed a Continental Congress to address their grievances for the first time in 1774. At that time they did not so much want revolution or independence from England as to resolve their issues with the king and Parliament. When reconciliation failed, the American Revolution began.

The American Revolution and Declaration of Independence were firmly based on Enlightenment principles. Jefferson, as a member of a five-man committee, was the main author of the Declaration of Independence. Committee members John Adams and Benjamin Franklin—also enlightened thinkers—added to the document, which was slightly modified and passed by the Continental Congress on July 4, 1776. The supremacy of enlightened reason is represented by the concept of self-evident truths in the opening statement. The ideas of the equality of men and their natural, inalienable rights come from Locke, as does the statement that governments derive their power from the consent of the governed. Kieron O'Hara says, "America declared itself independent with great statements of the centrality of human rights and self-government, using the language and concepts of the liberal tradition of the Enlightenment."[47]

American colonists and British soldiers exchange fire at the Battle of Lexington, the first skirmish in the Revolutionary War. The American Revolution, based on Enlightenment principles, provided a model for how to organize a democratic society.

The American Revolution was perhaps the pinnacle of Enlightenment thinking. Historian Henry J. Sage explains,

The Revolution was more than just a protest against English authority; as it turned out, the American Revolution provided a blueprint for the organization of a democratic society. And while imperfectly done, for it did not address the terrible problem of slavery, the American Revolution was an enlightened concept of government whose most profound documents may have been the American Declaration of Independence and United States Constitution. . . . While the locus of the Enlightenment thinking is generally considered to have been the salons in Paris and

Berlin, the practical application of those ideas was carried out most vividly in the American colonies.[48]

Enlightened but Carefully So

Yet, for all the radicalism of the American Revolution, the organization of the government as set by the US Constitution was basically a conservative one. The ideals were Enlightenment liberal ideals, but they were applied conservatively, maintaining traditions and cultural values. The new government was not a democracy because the founders feared rule by the many. It was a republic, in which representatives of the people would make the laws, thus ensuring—they hoped— that reason would determine the rule of law, not the unenlightened passions of a people with too much power. The government's authority came from the people, but the people did not control what the government did; they only would choose who their government representatives would be. At the same time, America's founders also feared a government with excessive power. From England they borrowed the idea of separate branches of government, with each being independent and having real influence to act as a check and balance on the others.

In 1787 and 1788 a series of anonymous newspaper articles were published that promoted the ratification of a new Constitution. Historian Richard B. Morris says the series of articles are "an incomparable exposition of the Constitution."[49] The series is known as the *Federalist Papers* and laid out the ideals upon which the Constitution was based and why it deserved to be approved by the states. O'Hara explains, "Actually written by James Madison, Alexander Hamilton and John Jay, they tried to design a representative government strong enough to levy taxes and defend the nation, subtle enough not to be ensnared by factions, yet not powerful enough to threaten hard-won liberty."[50] Madison, in particular, saw the Constitution as the means to use reason as the guiding political force of the new nation. The United States was choosing a moderately conservative form of government that would exemplify Enlightenment ideals.

The conservative, reasonable approach of America's founders was admired and approved by many Enlightenment thinkers. In England, Irish Member of Parliament Edmund Burke had supported the goals of the American Revolution. He argued that the colonies were too far away to be adequately represented in the English Parliament and that England should not tax them without representation. Although he hoped that the Americans would remain with England, he also

The French Declaration of the Rights of Man and the Citizen

The Declaration of the Rights of Man and the Citizen was approved by the National Assembly of France on August 26, 1789. It includes seventeen articles of duties, principles, and rights. Its opening statement reads:

> The representatives of the French people, constituted as a National Assembly, and considering that ignorance, neglect, or contempt of the rights of man are the sole causes of public misfortunes and governmental corruption, have resolved to set forth in a solemn declaration the natural, inalienable and sacred rights of man: so that by being constantly present to all the members of the social body this declaration may always remind them of their rights and duties; so that by being liable at every moment to comparison with the aim of any and all political institutions the acts of the legislative and executive powers may be the more fully respected; and so that by being founded henceforward on simple and incontestable principles the demands of the citizens may always tend toward maintaining the constitution and the general welfare.

"Declaration of the Rights of Man—1789," Avalon Project, Lillian Goldman Law Library, Yale Law School, 2008. http://avalon.law.yale.edu.

recognized that elected representatives were necessary for liberty and eventually supported the American revolutionaries. Burke was an enlightened thinker, but conservatively, he condemned the idea of pure democracy and praised the moderate government of the United States. He believed in maintaining tradition and reforming society without completely overturning it for something new. More radical Enlightenment leaders disagreed.

Enlightenment and the French Revolution

The Enlightenment leaders in France, perhaps emboldened by the success of the American Revolution, saw revolution and transformation of government in their own country as the only way to eliminate the injustices of their oppressive monarchy. If a democratic republic could be successfully achieved in a country as large as America, they reasoned, then a revolution in France was possible as well. But their ideology was much more radical than that of America's Enlightenment thinkers.

One of the most influential of French Enlightenment thinkers was Jean-Jacques Rousseau, who famously said, "Men are born free, yet everywhere they are in chains."[51] Rousseau believed that freedom was humanity's natural state and that the only way people could keep that freedom in any society was by maintaining equality. This meant that all the people in that community would give up their individual rights to the collective will of society because they all had basic interests in common. The people would pool all their rights and be governed by a unified, rational will that Rousseau calls the *sovereign*. The *sovereign* is the general will of all the people and operates for the common good. Rousseau believed that the government of such a society could be a monarchy, rule by aristocracy, or a democracy. But whatever form it took, such a government cannot be wrong because the general will cannot be wrong.

After Rousseau's death in 1778 his ideas still had a tremendous impact on French thinking, especially his idea that the general will of the people cannot be wrong. During the 1780s French *philosophes* and Enlightenment leaders vigorously debated how best to achieve liberty.

While some were advocates of moderation and gradual reform of existing institutions as the best path to liberty, others argued that true freedom could be achieved only by a government that submitted to the will of the people. In 1789 a revolutionary assembly of representatives of the people of France—predominantly middle-class people with some enlightened aristocrats—gathered with the goal of drafting a constitution for the nation. The group was called the National Constituent Assembly, and it essentially coerced King Louis XVI and the powerful French aristocracy and clergy to accept its right to exist and demand reforms. One of the Assembly's first acts was to draft a declaration of Enlightenment values and basic human freedoms, known as The Declaration of the Rights of Man and the Citizen.

The Declaration of the Rights of Man and the Citizen maintains that each individual has natural, universal, and inalienable rights. It says that every person is equal, no matter what his class or status; that the law has to apply equally to all; that taxes have to be assessed equally; and that anything not forbidden by law is acceptable. It requires religious tolerance and the right to free speech. It includes a demand for the separation of governmental powers. It declares that law and government are legitimate only as a reflection of the general will of the people.

The declaration's human rights, however, did not apply to slaves or women. The French working class and peasants—the majority of the people—were not represented among the assembly delegates, either. A few delegates, including the liberal, enlightened Marie-Jean-Antoine-Nicolas de Caritat, Marquis de Condorcet, argued for the inclusion of women's rights, but they were voted down by the rest of the assembly. In this sense, the document might seem conservative, but in its repudiation of the nobility, the monarchy, and the clergy, it was a radical demand for change in authoritarian France, especially since it outlawed the feudal system upon which the aristocracy depended.

The Tyranny of the General Will

For their part, the privileged aristocracy and clergy had no intention of giving up their power, their elite positions, or their wealth. As the

The execution of King Louis XVI of France is depicted in this eighteenth-century engraving. The beheading was but one of thousands of executions carried out by guillotine during the French Revolution.

National Constituent Assembly spread its revolutionary message and the king's influence grew weaker, the general population—oppressed, heavily taxed, and suffering extreme poverty—rose up and rioted, looted, and attacked and killed the nobles and their representatives in the cities and the countryside. The old system of government was completely overthrown.

At first, in 1791, the National Constituent Assembly wrote a constitution that established a constitutional monarchy that was to protect the rights of all citizens, but to the more radical enlightened leaders, this type of government did not give enough power to the people. The leaders of the Revolution ended up divided into two factions. They were the moderate (or less radical) constitutional monarchists, called the Girondins, and the radical Jacobins, who hated Louis XVI and wanted a democratic republic. Both factions were enlightened thinkers, but their reason led them to two extremely different points of view.

The Girondins feared mob rule and the loss of traditional governmental institutions, while the Jacobins were determined to usher in the liberalism of the supremacy of the general will.

The Jacobins triumphed. The monarchy was abolished and a republic established. King Louis XVI was tried for treason and executed, as was his wife, Marie-Antoinette. In the name of the general will and to protect "pure democracy," the French nation was starting anew. The National Convention set up a new calendar and began a campaign to wipe out Christianity for its opposition to reason and reform.

Under the influence of Maximilien Robespierre, a major leader of the Revolution, France's Reign of Terror began in 1793. More than seventeen thousand people were executed because they opposed the excessive revolutionary goals of the new republic. Robespierre argued fiercely, "Subdue by terror the enemies of liberty, and you will be right, as founders of the Republic. The government of the revolution is liberty's despotism against tyranny."[52] The "general will," under which the state could do no wrong, had become a bloody, horrifying dictatorship. In 1794 a group of moderate Girondins and disaffected Jacobins revolted, took over the government, and arrested and executed Robespierre and twenty-one of his closest supporters. France's revolutionary democratic experiment failed, and within a few years General Napoléon Bonaparte staged a coup and declared himself emperor.

Gone Too Far?

In many ways the French Terror marked the end of the Enlightenment era. O'Hara explains, "Only in America, well away from the carnage, could an Enlightenment of sorts carry on, although a conservative and neutered Enlightenment which repudiated the French upheaval."[53] In Europe, general revulsion for the mindless bloodshed in France led many to fear that Enlightenment values were not politically feasible in their modern world.

Chapter 5

What Is the Legacy of the Enlightenment?

The Enlightenment era had both short-term and long-term effects on the culture, thinking, and politics of Europe and America. As the eighteenth century drew to a close, some opted for the security of tradition and religion rather than unconstrained liberty; others questioned the supremacy of reason; and still others had serious doubts about the basic goodness and morality of humanity. Nonetheless, enlightened thinking and knowledge did not disappear. Many modern historians and philosophers say that the Enlightenment never really ended at all. Its lasting legacy is the world we live in today.

In the Aftermath of the French Revolution

At the end of the eighteenth century and during the nineteenth century the violence and failure of the French Revolution led to a serious questioning of Enlightenment ideals. Many thinkers especially doubted the practicality of democracy, equality, and the use of reason as the way to revolutionize and remake society and create moral humans. Even as the Revolution was raging, Edmund Burke published *Reflections on the Revolution in France* in 1790, in which he criticized the extremism of the unrestrained attack upon France's government and religion.

Burke argued that the revolutionaries of France did not understand that liberty is not the only ideal of a civilized society. Conservatively, he insisted that unlimited freedom did not benefit any nation and that an unrestrained populace would destroy liberty rather than preserve it. When traditions and the moral force of religion and governmental institutions are abandoned, people become uncivilized animals who can be controlled only by brute force and thus lose the liberty they sought. Burke said, "To make a government requires no great prudence. Settle the seat of power; teach obedience and the work is done. To give freedom is still more easy. It is not necessary to guide; it only requires to let go the rein. But to form a *free government*; that is, to temper together these opposite elements of liberty and restraint in one consistent work, requires much thought, deep reflection, a sagacious, powerful, and combining mind. This I do not find in those who take the lead in the National Assembly [of France]. . . . The improvements of the National Assembly are superficial, their errors are fundamental."[54] Burke used his enlightened reason to condemn political reform that did not combine both liberty and constraint. It was why he praised the American Revolution but opposed the French Revolution.

Along with other skeptical Enlightenment thinkers, Burke believed that no individual's reason could be counted on to be accurate always. The excesses of the French Revolution demonstrated that reason could be fallible and never the sole determinant of even enlightened thought. Unlike such philosophers as Locke and Rousseau, Burke did not accept the existence of a universal reason or universal truths that applied to everyone in any society. This means that reason is not always objective, even for enlightened individuals. Burke argued that human nature, society, and culture are too complex for one standard to apply to all. People are born into a society, culture, family, religion, and economic situation that affects their reasoning. Emotions, experiences, and unconscious motivations are often more important than reasoning when people make choices. There is no one point of view that represents everyone.

Therefore the French revolutionaries, according to Burke, did not represent general will at all. They were middle-class people who had different values than French aristocrats or working-class people. Their destruction of the culture and traditions of their society was inevitably wrong because they ignored the traditions and morals that were an

Edmund Burke speaks to members of the British Parliament. Burke argued that unlimited freedom, far from being a societal benefit, would destroy liberty.

essential part of their country. Reasonable or not, these traditions and morals must be a central part of a successful political system.

Another who criticized the Revolution was the French priest Augustin Barruel. Barruel, who was exiled during the height of the Reign of Terror, was an anti-Enlightenment figure who railed against the Revolution and all French thinkers indiscriminately. He said that enlightened people, especially the Jacobins, were anti-Christian, anti-monarchal, and antisocial, and he claimed that they deliberately formed a vast conspiracy to destroy European civilization. He called them members of "sects" that aimed "to subvert the whole fabric of the Christian religion."[55]

Many people were in sympathy with Barruel's views, although few believed in a real conspiracy. Other religious leaders condemned the godlessness and anarchy of the Revolution as the logical result of Enlightenment thinking that was naïve and heretical in its efforts to replace God's morality with cold reason. Even American founder John Adams rejected the French attempt to enshrine reason as a secular religion. He commented, "I know not what to make of a republic of thirty million atheists."[56]

The Romantic Era

Immediately after the Enlightenment era, many people lost faith in the power and value of reason. The legitimacy of emotions—or passions— and religious values gained ascendency. Thus the literary, artistic, and intellectual movement known as the Romantic era was born.

Romanticism was a revolt during the first half of the nineteenth century against reason and science that instead emphasized intense emotion, imagination, and intuition as ways to understand humanity, life, and nature. This attitude did not mean that people abandoned reason, but they did come to believe that reason alone was not sufficient for understanding human nature. They still valued the individual, happiness, tolerance, and freedom, but they thought in terms of the meaningfulness of love and passion instead of detached intellectual observation. Politically, this attitude led to an increased appreciation of the cultural and folk traditions that defined each nation. Eventually it gave rise to a revived nationalism and patriotism throughout Europe and North America. In the arts and in religious beliefs, feelings, intuition, spirituality, and imagination became more important than logic and reason.

Artistic works during the Romantic period celebrated untamed nature, its power, and its unpredictability instead of depicting natural laws or order or attempting to educate or rationally inspire the viewer. Art, the Romantics thought, was meant to be subjective, not objective.

It might appeal to emotion only and depict humanity's struggle with nature rather than control of nature. Shipwrecks, for instance, were popular subjects as examples of human helplessness amidst nature's fury. Art historian Kathryn Calley Galitz of New York's Metropolitan Museum of Art explains,

> Scenes of shipwrecks culminated in 1819 with Théodore Gericault's strikingly original *Raft of the Medusa* (Louvre), based on a contemporary event. In its horrifying explicitness, emotional intensity, and conspicuous lack of a hero, the *Raft of the Medusa* became an icon of the emerging Romantic style. Similarly, J.M.W. Turner's 1812 depiction of Hannibal and his army crossing the Alps (Tate Britain, London), in which the general and his troops are dwarfed by the overwhelming scale of the landscape and engulfed in the swirling vortex of snow, embodies the Romantic sensibility in landscape painting.[57]

Emotion prevailed over reason in poetry and literature as well. Writers of the Romantic era celebrated any strong emotion, whether it was horror, grief, intense love, or the soul's intuitive oneness with God. In contrast to enlightened thinkers such as Voltaire, who hated what they called the "enthusiasm" of religious fervor or passionate spirituality, Romantic thinkers embraced that enthusiasm. The poet and artist William Blake, for example, fiercely rejected Enlightenment thinking. He attacked Newton's explanation of the universe and its natural laws as too mechanical. Newton, Blake thought, ignored God, spirituality, and emotion and therefore did not understand the universe at all. Blake once wrote, "He who sees the Infinite in all things, sees God. He who sees the Ratio only, sees himself only."[58] He caricatured Newton as a man obsessed with his compass, using math to define the universe, and never seeing the bigger picture of the meaning of anything in life. The poet Samuel Taylor Coleridge similarly criticized Enlightenment leaders such as Locke and Newton. Although he began as an Enlightenment thinker, Coleridge rejected enlightened values after the French Revolution. He came to believe that reason and understanding were two very

Margaret Fuller

Born in Massachusetts in 1810, Margaret Fuller was a central figure in the Transcendentalist movement begun by Ralph Waldo Emerson. She was a highly educated, intelligent woman who became a writer, journalist, educator, and political activist. In 1840 she and Emerson founded a journal named the *Dial* that was devoted to transcendental thought and included essays on topics such as political reform, intelligence, and religion and spirituality, as well as poetry and literary reviews. Between 1839 and 1844 she led a series of seminars for women—called "Conversations"—in Boston, in which she encouraged women to analyze and discuss various philosophical and political issues. It was an exciting experience for Boston's women, who usually found their opinions ignored when they did not revolve around home and children. In 1845 Fuller published a feminist tract, *Woman in the Nineteenth Century*, which was extremely critical of the way women were treated—both by their husbands and society. She argued for women's independence and their ability to think and act in any endeavor as well as men could. Fuller died tragically in a shipwreck in 1850, but she is remembered today as America's first true feminist.

different things. He argued that reality is spiritual and that reason alone cannot lead to full understanding of anything.

Romantic literature often rejected the optimism of the Enlightenment and instead reflected the complexity of the individual's personality and his or her emotional conflicts, both psychologically and within society. Mary Shelley's *Frankenstein*, written in 1818, is an example of both the horror and pessimism that could fascinate Romantic thinkers. Literature professor Eleanor Ty says of Dr. Frankenstein and the monster he creates, "Their relationship is similar to that between the head and the heart, or the intellect and the emotion. . . . Frankenstein and his monster alternately pursue and flee from one another. Like fragments of a mind in conflict with itself, they represent polar opposites which are not reconciled, and which destroy each other at the end."[59]

Transcendentalism

The Romantic Movement was about the value of the individual as much as the Enlightenment was, but it was about the individual as a whole instead of the supremacy of his or her reason. And it took many different and individual forms. In the United States a basically optimistic philosophy—Transcendentalism—represented post-Enlightenment thinking during the Romantic era. Transcendentalism is the philosophy that people have knowledge about the world that goes beyond (transcends) what their senses perceive (empiricism) and what they can logically reason out. Transcendentalists believe in intuition and spirituality as a way to understand life and God, even when they do not adhere to any organized religion. They believe that they can trust in their own intuition and spirituality to determine what is morally right. And they believe that God, or the divine, is present in all of nature and in human beings.

Perhaps the first and most influential of the transcendentalists was Ralph Waldo Emerson, who gave the movement its name. The term *transcendentalism* comes from the Enlightenment writings of Immanuel Kant, based on his statements that how people know about perceived objects *transcends* the objects themselves—that human understanding is more than what the senses perceive. But even as he admired Kant's philosophy, Emerson rejected European culture and argued for a uniquely American way of thinking. In an 1837 speech given at Harvard, he exemplified this vision when he said, "We will walk on our own feet; we will work with our own hands; we will speak our own minds. . . . A nation of men will for the first time exist, because each believes himself inspired by the Divine Soul which also inspires all men."[60]

Emerson's ideals inspired other American thinkers, and they eagerly embraced his vision of an ideal America. The transcendentalists were a progressive people who adhered to the ideas of feminism, abolition of slavery, communal living, and the innate goodness of all people. They believed that each individual could find beauty and truth by meditating, communing with nature, and understanding oneself. The philosophy emphasized the merits of individualism, self-reliance, and the unique goodness of the American spirit and culture.

Many of the transcendentalists' religious beliefs evolved from Unitarianism, a liberal religion that rejected the concept of original sin and united Enlightenment principles with Christianity. Unitarians used intellectual reason to find the path to God. The transcendentalists accepted some of these principles, but they were more spiritual and emotional in their theology. They accepted reason but did not think it sufficient to fully commune with God and nature. Some transcendentalists remained firmly Christian, some rejected organized religion, and others—such as Emerson—thought of God in more universal, non-Christian terms.

The Evangelical Movement

By the nineteenth century in Europe and America, religion and religious dogma no longer held the power it had before the Enlightenment. The superstition that had permeated Christianity was waning, and many religious groups incorporated reason into their faith. The excesses of religious intolerance that had led to religious wars and persecution had largely been replaced by enlightened tolerance and a true respect for each individual's right to seek God in his or her own way. Yet, in the United States, the horrors of the French Revolution, which were perpetrated in the name of reason, led to a revived belief that traditional religion was the only path to morality. Millions of Americans sought not transcendentalism but emotional religious experiences. In a revolt against secularism, people embraced evangelism and a purely emotional and spiritual Christianity.

This American evangelical Christian revival movement lasted from about 1800 to 1870. The movement was defined by mass religious meetings led by passionate, emotional preachers who urged conversion to Christian moral values and acceptance of God's love for each

A decades-old photograph shows the Reverend Billy Graham preaching to a crowd. Evangelicals such as Graham were influenced by Charles Grandison Finney, an evangelical preacher and social reformer whose emotional sermons convinced thousands of people to accept Christ.

individual. People often experienced religious ecstasies as they accepted Christ and felt God's love and promise of salvation. Faith, not reason, was the basis for conversion. One of the most influential of evangelistic preachers was Charles Grandison Finney, who held massive revivals throughout America and converted thousands of people with his message of God's love and the necessity of accepting Jesus in order to be saved. He also threatened his listeners with eternal damnation if they refused to obey the Christian message.

Finney was a fierce social reformer, and in the name of Christianity he condemned alcohol, slavery, and treating women as second-class citizens. Through his emotional evangelism he hoped to cleanse America of its sins. Historian James E. Johnson says, "Charles Finney made a significant impression upon the religious life of 19th century America, and his influence is still evident today. Called the 'father of modern revivalism' by some historians, he paved the way for later revivalists like Dwight L. Moody, Billy Sunday, and Billy Graham. . . . Just as the American frontier was being widened and common folk were getting the vote, Finney gave the public an opportunity to cast their votes on the matter of salvation."[61] Eventually, Finney became president of Oberlin College in Ohio—the first college to admit women and African Americans and a hotbed of abolitionism before the American Civil War.

Conservative religious leaders often criticized Finney and other evangelicals for their emotionalism and fervor, but the evangelical beliefs in individual rights, human equality, and social morality—all actually a legacy of the Enlightenment—did more to reform the iniquities of the time than did the calm, reasoning intellectuals. The evangelical Christian William Wilberforce, for example, was an English member of Parliament whose faith led him to struggle for the abolition of the British Empire's slave trade. During the Enlightenment, its leaders sometimes intellectually opposed slavery as against reason, but they did nothing about it. Wilberforce fought a passionate campaign to end the slave trade, which finally succeeded in England in 1807, although slavery was not banned until 1833. His antislavery stance was based on his Christian morality, not on reason or philosophy. He once said, "When men are devoid of religion, I see that they are not to be relied on."[62]

Enduring Legacy and Conflict

The tension between reason and faith never really disappeared, just as the Enlightenment division between conservative and liberal thought has persisted in Western culture. In the long term, both the Enlightenment and the reaction against some of its values continue to define European and American society in many ways. Enlightenment perspectives toward liberty, the individual, inalienable rights, religious tolerance, and reason are as much a part of modern thought as they were in the eighteenth century.

For some modern people the importance of reason, especially in the areas of science and organized religion, remains paramount. These thinkers still see reason and banishing ignorance and superstition as the best way to improve societies and the condition of humankind. For others, individualism, diversity of culture, and spiritual freedom are most important. They reject social demands for conformity to standard ways of thinking or living and often condemn rationality as inhumane and unable to address real human needs. In this way the Enlightenment debates continue. Kieron O'Hara says, "These two types of thinker have absorbed the Enlightenment tradition, although they have reacted to it differently, and are recognizable at various times in the two centuries and more since the [French] Revolution."[63] Many historians say that the Enlightenment era never died; it is a process that remains ongoing today.

Western civilization continues to put much of its trust in science and scientific knowledge to benefit humanity. During the nineteenth century, building on the empiricism of the Enlightenment era, explosive scientific and technological breakthroughs occurred. With inventions such as electric lights, telephones, subways, skyscrapers and ships built of modern steel, and motion pictures, the foundations of modern-day conveniences and comforts were born. In physics, John Dalton developed the first atomic theory of matter, and Marie and Pierre Curie discovered radioactivity. In biology, Charles Darwin formulated his theory of the evolution of species, and in medicine, Robert Koch proved the germ theory of disease. Sigmund Freud searched for a psychological explanation of human behavior and proposed the theory of the unconscious mind. At the beginning of the twentieth century Albert Einstein came up with

The Enlightened World Wide Web

According to historian Kieron O'Hara, the twentieth century's development of the World Wide Web is a prime example of the Enlightenment's legacy today. The World Wide Web is based on the ideals of liberty and tolerance. It is a place where anyone can say anything he or she wants and connect with anyone he or she chooses. No central governing body censors content or connectivity. Thus, information flows freely over the Internet. People can cooperate and collaborate and create opportunities for themselves. It is free trade and the free market without national borders. In theory, the World Wide Web can expand without limit.

In many ways, claims O'Hara, the Internet is Diderot's *Encyclopédie* grown unimaginably large—with all knowledge and information available to all people. Diderot wanted his encyclopedia to provide knowledge to anyone in any nation on Earth, and the Internet transcends international boundaries with ease. The World Wide Web is real democracy and a triumph of the free market in a true embodiment of enlightened ideals, although certainly, repressive governments have constrained and censored the Internet in their own countries. "Nevertheless," says O'Hara, "for the moment the World Wide Web remains the most visible and tangible, though virtual, manifestation of the Enlightenment project."

Kieron O'Hara, *The Enlightenment*, Beginner's Guides. Oxford, UK: Oneworld, 2010, p. 209.

the theory of relativity, which explains the physics of the universe that could not be explained by Newton. The liberal, optimistic Enlightenment belief that humanity is on a steady upward climb of progress and perfectibility seemed validated by continual scientific progress.

Yet for some historians and philosophers science itself undermines Enlightenment thought. Freud's theories, for example, suggest that people often fail to make choices rationally. Instead, unconscious motivations and emotional issues may determine their behavior, even when they are unaware of it. This may mean that people do not make reasonable voting decisions, and so democracy and representative governments may not operate on the basis of reason at all. Evolutionary theories and subsequent genetic discoveries may indicate that individuals do not have the free will to base their actions on reason. Perhaps they are simply controlled by their genetic makeup and cannot have a meaningful impact on the world with their decisions. The universe, according to relativity theory, is not even as understandable and knowable as enlightened thinkers predicted it would be.

Cold, unfeeling reason has also justified some horrors in the so-called civilized world. Some historians explain that the definition of reason can be twisted and subverted until it becomes irrational and immoral, as it did with Nazi ideology in Germany or the old Soviet Union's interpretation of communism that led to purges, repression, and gulags in the name of the collective will of the people. Other historians, however, see the Enlightenment's true legacy as a moral philosophical belief system of universal tolerance, equality, individual liberty, and a democratic republicanism as the best form of government, whatever its possible flaws.

Still Seeking Enlightenment

Reason and tolerance may not be the answer to all of humankind's problems, but arguably they have made the world a better place for more people than any other philosophical system. What is the legacy of the Enlightenment? In a very real sense the answer is as controversial today as it was during the eighteenth century. People continue to ask what enlightenment means, how an individual becomes enlightened, and what an enlightened civilization looks like. In 1795 the French philosopher Marie-Jean-Antoine-Nicolas de Caritat, Marquis de Condorcet wrote, "The time will come when the sun will shine only on free men who have no master but their reason."[64] If he is right, the Enlightenment is still a work in progress.

Source Notes

Introduction: The Defining Characteristics of the Enlightenment

1. Immanuel Kant, "What Is Enlightenment?," in "Kant on Enlightenment, the Making of the Modern Mind," Manchester College. www.manchester.edu.
2. Kieron O'Hara, *The Enlightenment*, Beginner's Guides. Oxford, UK: Oneworld, 2010, p. 96.
3. Quoted in Robert E. Schofield, *The Enlightenment of Joseph Priestley: A Study of His Life and Work from 1733 to 1773*. University Park, PA: Pennsylvania State University Press, 1997, p. 209.

Chapter One: What Conditions Led to the Enlightenment?

4. Judith M. Bennett and C. Warren Hollister, *Medieval Europe: A Short History*, 10th ed. New York: McGraw-Hill, 2006, p. 2.
5. Bennett and Hollister, *Medieval Europe*, p. 289.
6. Quoted in Jeremiah Hackett, "Roger Bacon," *The Stanford Encyclopedia of Philosophy*, Winter 2013, Edward N. Zalta, ed., Stanford University. http://plato.stanford.edu.
7. Quoted in Hackett, "Roger Bacon."
8. Francesco Petrarch, "Francesco Petrarch to Posterity," Letters: Francesco Petrarch & Laura deNoves, Peter Sadlon, September 10, 2007. http://petrarch.petersadlon.com.
9. Quoted in Charline Tiller, "Erasmus of the Renaissance," Mr. Renaissance, 2002. www.mrrena.com.
10. Quoted in Victoria Rahn, "Erasmus' Praise of Folly: A Renaissance Work," Wisconsin Lutheran College, April 2002, p. 7. www.charis.wlc.edu.
11. Quoted in A&E Networks, "Nicolaus Copernicus: Biography," 2014, p. 3. www.biography.com.
12. O'Hara, *The Enlightenment*, Beginner's Guides, p. 41.
13. O'Hara, *The Enlightenment*, Beginner's Guides, p. 42.

14. Quoted in Asa Kasher and Shlomo Biderman, "Why Was Baruch de Spinoza Excommunicated?," in David S. Katz and Jonathan I. Israel, eds., *Sceptics, Millenarians and Jews*. Leiden, Netherlands: E.J. Brill, 1990, p. 133.

Chapter Two: Enlightenment Philosophy and Religion

15. Robert A. Hatch, "Sir Isaac Newton," University of Florida, 1998. http://web.clas.ufl.edu.
16. Quoted in Steve Connor, "The Core of Truth Behind Sir Isaac Newton's Apple," *Independent* (UK), January 18, 2010. www.independent.co.uk.
17. Quoted in Connor, "The Core of Truth Behind Sir Isaac Newton's Apple."
18. Hatch, "Sir Isaac Newton."
19. Quoted in James Ford and Mary Ford, eds., "March 21: Epitaph on Sir Isaac Newton," Bartleby.com. www.bartleby.com.
20. O'Hara, *The Enlightenment*, Beginner's Guides, p. 51.
21. Ian Mertes, Bob Manzano, and Bill Cross, "John Locke," Keith Millis, History of Psychology, Northern Illinois University, 2003. www3.niu.edu.
22. John Locke, *An Essay Concerning Human Understanding*, 30th ed. London: William Tegg & Co., Cheapside, 1849, p. 53.
23. Claude Adrien Helvetius, in "Claude Adrien Helvetius—Quotes," European Graduate School. www.egs.edu.
24. Quoted in O'Hara, *The Enlightenment*, Beginner's Guides, p. 61.
25. Quoted in Ryan Pevnick, "The Lockean Case for Religious Tolerance: The Social Contract and the Irrationality of Persecution," *Political Studies*, vol. 57, New York University, 2009, p. 851. www.politics.as.nyu.edu.
26. Voltaire, in *The Philosophical Dictionary*, trans. H.I. Woolf. New York: Knopf, 1924, Hanover Historical Texts Project, Hanover College Department of History. https://history.hanover.edu.
27. Steven Kreis, "Lecture 9: Écrasez l'infâme! The Triumph of Science and the Heavenly City of the 18th Century *Philosophe*," History Guide, 2000. www.historyguide.org.
28. Quoted in Dorinda Outram, *The Enlightenment*, 3rd ed. New York: Cambridge University Press, 2013, p. 2.
29. Quoted in Neil Duxbury, "Golden Rule Reasoning, Moral Judgment and Law," University of Virginia School of Law, p. 26. www.law.virginia.edu.

30. Peter S. Onuf, "Thomas Jefferson and Deism," Gilder Lehrman Institute of American History. www.gilderlehrman.org.

31. Quoted in Onuf, "Thomas Jefferson and Deism."

32. Quoted in Onuf, "Thomas Jefferson and Deism."

Chapter Three: Enlightenment Arts and Science

33. O'Hara, *The Enlightenment*, Beginner's Guides, p. 162.

34. Quoted in O'Hara, *The Enlightenment*, Beginner's Guides, p. 167.

35. Voltaire, *Candide*. Rockville, MD: Wildside Press, 2007, p. 43.

36. Quoted in Donald J. Mabry, "Diderot's Encyclopedia," Historical Text Archive. http://historicaltextarchive.com.

37. Martin Schönfeld, "Kant's Philosophical Development," *Stanford Encyclopedia of Philosophy*, Edward N. Zalta, ed., Stanford University, January 18, 2007. http://plato.stanford.edu.

38. Understanding Evolution, "Old Earth, Ancient Life: Georges-Louis Leclerc, Comte de Buffon," University of California at Berkeley. http://evolution.berkeley.edu.

39. Quoted in Robert M. Martin, *Scientific Thinking*. Toronto, ON: Broadview, 2000, p. 216.

40. Quoted in Martin, *Scientific Thinking*, p. 218.

41. Outram, *The Enlightenment*, pp. 112–13.

Chapter Four: Enlightenment Politics and Revolution

42. Quoted in Lonnie R. Johnson, *Central Europe: Enemies, Neighbors, Friends*. New York: Oxford University Press, 1996, p. 121.

43. Quoted in Larry Wolff, "'If I Were Younger I Would Make Myself Russian': Voltaire's Encounter with the Czars,'" *New York Times*, November 13, 1994. www.nytimes.com.

44. Quoted in O'Hara, *The Enlightenment*, Beginner's Guides, p. 100.

45. Quoted in Outram, *The Enlightenment*, p. 26.

46. John Locke, *Second Treatise of Government*, reproduced in Harvard University's Justice with Michael Sandel. www.justiceharvard.org.

47. O'Hara, *The Enlightenment*, Beginner's Guides, p. 73.

48. Henry J. Sage, "The Enlightenment in America," Sage American History, August 27, 2013. http://resources.saylor.org.

49. Quoted in Jim Willis, *100 Media Moments That Changed America*. Santa Barbara, CA: Greenwood, 2010, p. 10.

50. O'Hara, *The Enlightenment*, Beginner's Guides, p. 102.

51. Quoted in Christopher Bertram, "Jean Jacques Rousseau," *The Stanford Encyclopedia of Philosophy*, Edward N. Zalta, ed., Winter 2012, Stanford University. http://plato.stanford.edu.

52. Quoted in Paul Halsall, "Maximilien Robespierre: Justification of the Use of Terror," Modern History Sourcebook, Fordham University, August 1997. www.fordham.edu.

53. O'Hara, *The Enlightenment*, Beginner's Guides, p. 113.

Chapter Five: What Is the Legacy of the Enlightenment?

54. Quoted in Steven Kreis, "Edmund Burke, *Reflections on the Revolution in France* (1790)," Lectures on Modern European Intellectual History, The History Guide, 2001. www.historyguide.org.

55. Quoted in John Patrick Walsh, "Barruel, Augustin," Enlightenment and Revolution, April 29, 2008. http://enlightenment-revolution. org.

56. Quoted in David McCullough, *John Adams*. New York: Simon & Schuster Paperbacks, 2008, p. 418.

57. Kathryn Calley Galitz, "Romanticism," Heilbrunn Timeline of Art History, Metropolitan Museum of Art, October 2004. www.met museum.org.

58. William Blake, "There Is No Natural Religion," Bartleby.com. www .bartleby.com.

59. Eleanor Ty, "Mary Wollstonecraft Shelley," reprint, Andreas Teuber, Brandeis University. http://people.brandeis.edu.

60. Quoted in PBS.org, "The American Renaissance & Transcendentalism." www.pbs.org.

61. James E. Johnson, "Charles Grandison Finney: Father of American Revivalism," *Christian History*, no. 20, 1988, p. 4. www.christi anitytoday.com.

62. Quoted in Ermine Desmond, "A Force for Good: William Wilberforce and the End of Slavery," The Theologian, 2005. www.theolo gian.org.uk.

63. O'Hara, *The Enlightenment*, Beginner's Guides, p. 180.

64. Quoted in Outram, *The Enlightenment*, p. 1.

Important People of the Enlightenment

Edmund Burke: Irish member of Great Britain's Parliament. Considered the father of modern conservatism, Burke advocated a moderate, enlightened approach to political and social reform.

Denis Diderot: French philosopher and writer who was the driving force behind the publication of the massive *Encyclopédie* project, which resulted in one of the most important books of the Enlightenment era. Its goal was to increase knowledge, disseminate Enlightenment ideals, and combat the traditional power of church and state.

Benjamin Franklin: One of America's foremost founding fathers, Franklin was instrumental in introducing Enlightenment ideals to the American colonies and laying the foundations for political revolution. He also contributed to the development of the natural sciences in his pursuit of knowledge for the public good and participated in the Constitutional Convention of 1787.

Thomas Jefferson: American founding father who believed deeply in the Enlightenment principles of liberty, equality, and natural human rights. He was the principal author of the Declaration of Independence and subsequently was influential in helping to define the powers of the Constitution and the nature of the new republic of the United States.

Immanuel Kant: German philosopher central to Enlightenment and modern thought. He explicated rationalism and empiricism and logically argued that each individual's independent thought and experiences are the legitimate basis for all knowledge, understanding of natural laws, and morality, with reason and perception operating together to produce truth.

John Locke: English philosopher who developed and published theories on legitimate government existing only with the consent of the governed and on the natural, inalienable rights of each individual. Locke postulated the theory that humans are born innocent with their minds "blank slates," each equal to every other and different only because of the experiences and education they receive. He advocated religious tolerance, freedom for every individual, universal civil rights, and majority rule in society.

James Madison: The father of the US Constitution and one of the authors of the *Federalist Papers*. His ideas were instrumental in formulating a Constitution that was moderately conservative and ensured that no branch of government or majority decision could overly limit freedom or gain too much power.

Charles-Louis de Secondat, Baron de La Brède et de Montesquieu: Montesquieu was a major French philosopher who advocated governmental separation of powers in a constitutional monarchy that would ensure individual rights while limiting excessive freedom that innately selfish human beings might abuse in any society. His ideas had a direct influence on the US Constitution.

Wolfgang Amadeus Mozart: The musical genius and composer of the Enlightenment era. His extraordinarily complex opera *The Marriage of Figaro* was a tremendous success with its Enlightenment themes of social injustices and liberal ideas about individual equality and reason. His music influenced many later composers of the nineteenth and twentieth centuries.

Isaac Newton: Considered one of the greatest scientists who ever lived, Newton ushered in the Enlightenment era with his explication of the natural laws of motion and his theory of universal gravitation.

Jean-Jacques Rousseau: A radical French philosopher who argued for individual freedom and equality that could be expressed only in a democratic government that represented the "general will" of all the people. He said that in any good society, people voluntarily had to surrender their individual rights and pool them with the other individuals in the community to achieve true equality. Thus, obeying the general will was obeying oneself, and this was real freedom. Rousseau's theories had a great influence on the French Revolution.

Adam Smith: Scottish philosopher and economic theorist who advocated free-market economics in which the "invisible hand" of an unregulated system controls supply and demand to the benefit of all. Smith's *An Inquiry into the Nature and Causes of the Wealth of Nations*, published in 1776, is one of the most influential books of the Enlightenment. It is the basis of capitalism and modern economics.

Voltaire: The pen name of Francois-Marie Arouet, a French writer and philosopher. Through his literary works and satires, Voltaire crusaded against superstition, ignorance, governmental injustices, and religious intolerance. His works popularized Enlightenment ideals throughout Europe and America, even as he criticized enlightened thinkers who did not act upon their ideals.

For Further Research

Books

Fred Bortz, *Laws of Motion and Isaac Newton*. New York: Rosen, 2014.

John C. Davenport, *The French Revolution and the Rise of Napoleon*. New York: Chelsea House, 2011.

Josh Gregory, *The French Revolution*. Danbury, CT: Scholastic, 2013.

Thomas Jefferson, *The Jefferson Bible*. Aspen, CO: Independence Press, 2013.

Kathleen Krull, *Benjamin Franklin*. New York: Viking Children's Books, 2013.

Hal Marcovitz, *The Declaration of Independence*. San Diego: ReferencePoint, 2014.

Jon Meacham, *Thomas Jefferson: President and Philosopher*. New York: Crown Books for Young Readers, 2014.

Kenneth Pletcher, ed. *Explorers of the Late Renaissance and the Enlightenment: From Sir Francis Drake to Mungo Park*. New York: Rosen, 2013.

Marcus Weeks, *Mozart: The Boy Who Changed the World with his Music*. Des Moines, IA: National Geographic Children's Books, 2013.

Websites

ConstitutionFacts.com (www.constitutionfacts.com). At this very large site, visitors can read in detail about the Constitution, the Declaration of Independence, the founding fathers, and more. Take the fun quiz to test your knowledge of the Constitution.

The Discover John Locke Project (http://discoverjohnlocke.com/in dex.html). This Australian site is dedicated to John Locke—his life, his ideas, and his writings.

The Encyclopedia of Diderot & d'Alembert (http://quod.lib.umich .edu/d/did). This project consists of translated articles from the original *Encyclopédie* published in the eighteenth century. Visitors can browse the entries, search for specific entries, and view the original engraved plates that illustrated articles.

The Enlightenment (www3.gettysburg.edu/~tshannon/hist106web/ site6/enlightenment_front_page.htm). This website was compiled by students at Gettysburg College and covers in detail various aspects of the Enlightenment in Europe and the Americas. Major Enlightenment thinkers are described along with their contributions.

French Revolution: History.com (www.history.com/topics/french-rev olution). Watch and listen to musician and artist Jeffrey Lewis sing a brief and delightful history of the French Revolution. Other more conventional videos discuss the origins of the revolution and Robespierre's Reign of Terror.

Jean-Antoine Watteau (www.jean-antoine-watteau.org). Watteau was the artist who founded the rococo movement. At this website, visitors can view his complete works individually or watch a slide show of some 220 paintings. Click the Biography link to read about his life.

Law for Kids (www.lawforkids.org/Laws). Choose the link for Laws, then Law Documents and browse the Declaration of Independence, the US Constitution, the Bill of Rights, and the Federalist Papers.

Monticello.org (www.monticello.org/site/about). This is the official website of Thomas Jefferson's historic plantation, run by the Thomas Jefferson Foundation. The site includes many links describing Jefferson's life, his works, and his contributions.

The Newton Project (www.newtonproject.sussex.ac.uk/prism .php?id=1). This British website is dedicated to Sir Isaac Newton. It includes extensive articles about the man as well as online editions of his scientific and mathematical works, his notebooks, sketches, and personal letters.

Index

as constitutional monarchs, 56–57, 60–61
divine right of, 11, 34, 57
as enlightened monarchs, **58**, 59–61
feudalism and, 16
Koch, Robert, 80
Kratter, Franz, 61
Kreis, Steven, 38

Last Supper (da Vinci), 16
laws of motion, 29–30
Leclerc, Georges-Louis, 52
leisure time, 25–26
Leonardo da Vinci, 16
Leyden jar, 54
liberalism, 56
Linnaeus, Carl, 52, **53**, 54
Lisbon, Portugal, 49
literature
    Enlightenment
        Encyclopédie, 47, **48**, 49, 81
        novels, 44, 46
        poetry, 45
    Romantic Era, 74–76
Locke, John
    American Revolution and, 62
    Bayle and, 32
    belief in God, 38
    on government, 61
    ideas about natural laws of the mind, 33–34
Louis XV (king of France), 47, 58
Louis XVI (king of France), 67, 68, **68**, 69
Luther, Martin, 27

Madison, James, 64
Magellan, Ferdinand, 25
magic, 36
Magic Flute, The (Mozart), 44
manorial system, 17
Man's a Man for A' That, A (Burns), 45
Marie-Antoinette (queen of France), 68–69
Marriage of Figaro, The (Mozart), 44
Middle Ages (476–1450 CE), 15–17, 22–23
Millis, Keith, 33
mind, theories of, 26, 27, 33
miracles, 38
Moll Flanders (Defoe), 44, 46
Mona Lisa (da Vinci), 16
monarchies
    absolute, 27, 57–59, 61
    constitutional, 56–57, 60–61
    enlightened, **58**, 59–61
Montesquieu, Baron de La Brède et de, 61
morality without religion, 32, 36, 39
Morris, Richard B., 64
Mozart, Wolfgang Amadeus, 44
music, 44

Napoleon Bonaparte, 69
National Constituent Assembly (France), 68
natural laws
    improvements in life and, 41
    Locke, on 33–34
    natural disasters and, 18–19, 49
    Newton, on 30–31
    religion and, 38–39, 40, 45
    Voltaire, on 36
natural philosophy. *See* science

neoclassical art, 42–44, **43**
Newton, Isaac, **31**
    on belief in God, 38
    Blake on, 74
    death of, 30
    empiricism, 33
    importance of, 28, 30–32
    influence of, on Locke, 33
    and laws of universal gravitation and of
        motion, 29–30
    Pope on, 30–31
New World of the Americas, discovery and
    exploration of, 25
novels, 44, 46, 75–76

obedience to state and religion, 11–12
Oberlin College, 79
O'Hara, Kieron
    on American Revolution, 62
    on Descartes, 26
    on Enlightenment tradition, 80
    on *Federalist Papers,* 64
    on French Revolution, 69
    on later Renaissance, 26
    on music during Enlightenment, 44
    on pursuit of happiness, 34
    on science to explain natural events, 31–32
    on views about people of color, 11
    on World Wide Web, 81
Onuf, Peter S., 39–40
optimism, 13
Outram, Dorinda, 55

Paine, Thomas, 35, 39
Parlements, 57–58
peasants during Middle Ages, 17
people of color, 11
Petrarch, Francesco, 22–23
philosophe movement
    debates about liberty, 66–67
    described, 34
    Encyclopédie, 47, **48**, 49, 81
    religion and, 35, 36, 38–40
    Voltaire and, 36, **37**
Pilgrimage to the Island of Cythera (Watteau), 42
plague, 20
planets, knowledge about, 25, 29–30
poetry, 45, 74–75
politics. *See* government systems
Pombal, Marquis of, 55
Pope, Alexander, 30–31, 45
"Posterity" (Petrarch), 22–23
Praise of Folly, The (Erasmus), 23
Priestley, Joseph, 13
Prince of the Humanists (Erasmus), 23
Principia Mathematica (Newton), 28
protectionism, 60
Protestant Reformation, 21, 27

Raft of the Medusa (Gericault), 74
reason
    children and, 33–34
    in Deism, 35
    development of science and, 41
    in Enlightenment tradition currently, 80
    Freud's unconscious and, 82
    given by God to humans, 19, 39

About the Author

Toney Allman holds degrees from Ohio State University and the University of Hawaii. She currently lives in Virginia, where she enjoys a rural lifestyle as well as researching and writing about a variety of topics for students.

FRIENDS FREE LIBRARY
GERMANTOWN FRIENDS LIBRARY
5418 Germantown Avenue
Philadelphia, PA 19144
215-951-2355

Each borrower is responsible for all items
checked out on his/her library card, for
fines on materials kept overtime, and
replacing any lost or damaged materials.